MW00478710

Praise for *The Visibility Mindset*

"Finally, a much-needed handbook for the Asian American community and allies. I'm thrilled to have a single resource for students, faculty, and practitioners to learn how to thrive in, compete in, and navigate the workplace. As an educator, I'll be assigning this book. Kudos to Chao and Lam!"

—Robin Landa,
Distinguished Professor of Design, Kean University,
author of *The New Art of Ideas*

"Jessalin Lam and Bernice Chao clearly articulate how successful Asian Americans stay visible and present as they advance professionally. Their personal stories, timely advice, and thought-provoking interviews offer readers clear reasons why we should all embrace a mindset that focuses on being seen, heard, and valued. I encourage everyone to pick up a copy of this book and share it with others."

—Bill Imada,
founder and chairman, IW Group, Inc.

"Climbing the career ladder can be a lonely and overwhelming experience. Bernice and Jessalin have distilled the hard-learned lessons of those coming before us into relatable stories and practical strategies."

—Gorick Ng,
Wall Street Journal bestselling author of
The Unspoken Rules

"Jessalin and Bernice have written a remarkable and essential piece of work for current and future Asian Americans. From unpacking what it means to be an Asian American to providing critical and radical self-reflection tools, the powerhouse pair has developed an incredible foundation to break the bamboo ceiling and stereotypes imposed on us by society. Recognizable stories of microaggressions, being overlooked, and never being good enough, Jessalin and Bernice blend history with actionable steps that we can use to resist and disrupt the stereotypes that chain us down. *The Visibility Mindset: How Asian American Leaders Create Opportunities and Push Past Barriers* is a must for all Asian Americans advocating for social justice that recognizes and supports our community's unique talents."

—Christian Wu,
educational researcher and educator

"As a disability advocate who is also in the AAPI community, I recommend this book for anyone in the AAPI community and those who support, care about, and love us (our allies). The book includes tactical resources and lessons on improving yourself, overcoming stereotypes, and redefining the future of work. A must-read for all leaders and must-have on your bookshelf!"

—Tiffany Yu,
Founder and CEO, Diversability,
Ex Goldman Sachs, Bloomberg, REVOLT TV

"What a brilliant and clear way to explain the years of feeling a sense of "unbelonging" as growing up as an Asian American woman. These authors break down how to navigate through Asian American stereotypes and myths—I'm so glad there will be a tool for our future generations to figure out their voices and their roles in society."

—Mayly Tao,
Founder/CEO, Donut Princess LA and
author of *An American Dream, with Sprinkles:
The Legacy Story of the Donut Queen & Donut Princess*

"Jessalin Lam and Bernice Chao have written the MUST-READ handbook, not just for Asian Americans in business, but for Asians in business anywhere—and, quite frankly, for anyone who considers themselves an ally and a supporter of diversity and inclusion in the workplace. This insightful, practical, actionable guide will turbocharge your path to leadership—and to better business outcomes for all as a result."

—Cindy Gallop,
consultant and founder/CEO, MakeLoveNotPorn

"A powerful and inspiring book that will benefit everyone who implements it, an invaluable resource both for Asian Americans and allies! *The Visibility Mindset* is a treasure trove of principles, methods, and concepts that can elevate your life and career."

—Angela Marie,
Hutchinson, showrunner, screenwriter, and author of
*Create Your Yes! When You Keep Hearing NO: A 12-Step
Strategy for Success*

"This is an extremely effective book written by Jessalin and Bernice highlighting the nuisances and struggles of the Asian American diaspora. Jessalin and Bernice are leaders within the AAPI community and offer insight on how to cultivate, visualize and strategize for success. Keep reading from end to end, you won't be disappointed."

—Bryan Pham,
founder and CEO, Asian Hustle Network

"A must-read if you're ready to unlock your full potential! Bernice and Jessalin have written a manual for how to have the life and career you always imagined. You'll keep going back to this book for takeaways and action points. No matter your gender, race, age, and no matter what industry you are in, this book has something for you."

—**Tiffany Pham,**
CEO, Mogul

"Bernice and Jessalin's book is a resounding inspiration. Not only did it communicate how I can be an ally to AAPI, but it also spoke to me directly as a woman, empowering me on my own career path. A must-read for all creatives."

—**Rachel Rabin,**
"RAIGN," singer, songwriter, and founder of
Millionaire London Records

"Bernice and Jessalin have done a phenomenal job with this book by giving practical tips that anybody can use to become a leader. As someone who encourages our AAPI community to speak up, I know it can be challenging due to our cultural upbringing, and this book can help you come out of your shell. This book is a must-read and a great guide to finding your voice in your business and career."

—**Sheena Yap Chan,**
host of *The Tao of Self Confidence* and author of *Asian Women Who Boss Up*

THE
VISIBILITY
MINDSET

HOW ASIAN AMERICAN LEADERS CREATE
OPPORTUNITIES AND PUSH PAST BARRIERS

THE VISIBILITY MINDSET

BERNICE CHAO | JESSALIN LAM

WILEY

Copyright © 2023 by John Wiley & Sons, Inc. All rights reserved.

Published by John Wiley & Sons, Inc., Hoboken, New Jersey.
Published simultaneously in Canada.

No part of this publication may be reproduced, stored in a retrieval system, or transmitted in any form or by any means, electronic, mechanical, photocopying, recording, scanning, or otherwise, except as permitted under Section 107 or 108 of the 1976 United States Copyright Act, without either the prior written permission of the Publisher, or authorization through payment of the appropriate per-copy fee to the Copyright Clearance Center, Inc., 222 Rosewood Drive, Danvers, MA 01923, (978) 750-8400, fax (978) 646-8600, or on the Web at www.copyright.com. Requests to the Publisher for permission should be addressed to the Permissions Department, John Wiley & Sons, Inc., 111 River Street, Hoboken, NJ 07030, (201) 748-6011, fax (201) 748-6008, or online at http://www.wiley.com/go/permissions.

Trademarks: Wiley and the Wiley logo are trademarks or registered trademarks of John Wiley & Sons, Inc. and/or its affiliates in the United States and other countries and may not be used without written permission. All other trademarks are the property of their respective owners. John Wiley & Sons, Inc. is not associated with any product or vendor mentioned in this book.

Limit of Liability/Disclaimer of Warranty: While the publisher and author have used their best efforts in preparing this book, they make no representations or warranties with respect to the accuracy or completeness of the contents of this book and specifically disclaim any implied warranties of merchantability or fitness for a particular purpose. No warranty may be created or extended by sales representatives or written sales materials. The advice and strategies contained herein may not be suitable for your situation. You should consult with a professional where appropriate. Neither the publisher nor author shall be liable for any loss of profit or any other commercial damages, including but not limited to special, incidental, consequential, or other damages.

For general information on our other products and services or for technical support, please contact our Customer Care Department within the United States at (800) 762-2974, outside the United States at (317) 572-3993 or fax (317) 572-4002.

Wiley publishes in a variety of print and electronic formats and by print-on-demand. Some material included with standard print versions of this book may not be included in e-books or in print-on-demand. If this book refers to media such as a CD or DVD that is not included in the version you purchased, you may download this material at http://booksupport.wiley.com. For more information about Wiley products, visit www.wiley.com.

Library of Congress Cataloging-in-Publication Data

Names: Chao, Bernice M., author. | Lam, Jessalin, author.
Title: The visibility mindset : how Asian American leaders create
  opportunities and push past barriers / Bernice M. Chao and Jessalin Lam.
Description: First edition. | Hoboken, New Jersey : Wiley, [2023] |
  Includes index.
Identifiers: LCCN 2022032474 (print) | LCCN 2022032475 (ebook) | ISBN
  9781119890492 (cloth) | ISBN 9781119890812 (adobe pdf) | ISBN
  9781119890508 (epub)
Subjects: LCSH: Leadership—United States. | Career development—United
  States. | Asian Americans—Social conditions.
Classification: LCC BF637.L4 C433 2023 (print) | LCC BF637.L4 (ebook) |
  DDC 158/.4—dc23/eng/20220914
LC record available at https://lccn.loc.gov/2022032474
LC ebook record available at https://lccn.loc.gov/2022032475

Cover Design: IVAN KATHIA FELIZ GESTIADA / 99designs.com
Cover Image: © kinggodarts/Pixabay

SKY10036131_092222

To our incredible families for believing in us, to friends and community for their unconditional support, and to those who want to take a seat for themselves at the table.

Contents

Introduction

OUR STORY IS a commonly shared one. We are Asian Americans born in and living in the United States. While we are part of the American culture, we are still balancing the culture of our ethnic origin. We speak English fluently, but because of the differences in how we look, we are often seen as not quite "American" enough and since we are not being raised in our origin country, oftentimes, we are also not "Asian" enough. Throughout this book, we will be using the term *Asian Americans* to include all individuals of Asian descent but recognize that there are many other terms that can be used to mean the same thing, including *Asian American Pacific Islander* (AAPI) and often simply *Asian*.

Speaking generally, Asian parents teach us that we will succeed if we work hard. However, most of us know that hard work in this day and age is just not enough to succeed. We've learned that working hard usually means getting assigned more work instead of praise, raises, or promotions. We see others who did not put the same hours and dedication into their workload as we did, and they excel and get promoted without a clear explanation as to why. We look around and see those of Asian American descent leaving their corporations and starting their entrepreneurial endeavors because they couldn't work within the established system. Asian Americans are often not given the opportunities they deserve in the workplace, and we are here to break down these stereotypes and myths to help guide you through the challenges you may face along your career journey.

The two of us spent our careers in advertising and media, and we both were faced with the same upward momentum challenges. Through many years of struggling to be seen, we realized that we needed to apply what we knew from our work to ourselves in order to succeed. We realized that the same things that gain brands presence and recognition could also work for us. We found that rather than being passed over for opportunities, by implementing a brand strategy for ourselves, a new world of potential could open up to us, and we wanted to share this realization with others.

We created a nonprofit organization called Asians in Advertising to help advance Asian Americans into the c-suite. We did this by hosting community networking classes, spotlighting Asian American talent, and creating practical, career-enhancing lessons based on what we learned from our experiences and industry leaders. As a result, we saw many in our community were using these pointers to get new jobs and advance in their careers. Asian Americans began reaching out to us from many different industries and from all areas of the world.

We quickly realized that career enhancement strategies were useful not only to Asian Americans in the advertising field but also to Asian Americans in all business roles. Our reach had expanded globally, so we decided we needed to share what we had learned and to spread knowledge from others who had figured out tips for visibility. This book lays out many actionable steps to help you become seen in the workplace and to facilitate the opening up of many more opportunities to you, possibilities that would not necessarily have been available to you before. In the beginning of each chapter, you will see that each one is written by one of us as we wanted to include the personal nature of our own experiences that led us to write those specific chapters and integrate our own stories and perspectives.

We created this book as a guide for Asian Americans and see this book being used as a resource in schools, organizations, employee resource groups, book clubs, and friend groups, among others. We want anyone who has felt that they lacked visibility in the workplace to be able to have the tools to be seen. This book will also be an essential guide for employers, managers, and anyone interested in diversity, equity, and inclusion. If you are a non-Asian reading this book, we appreciate you being an ally to our community. Nothing in this book is the silver bullet, but we have found common issues and shared solutions. Feel free to take as much or as little as you need from it.

Common Myths

Before we go into what we have the potential to do, it is important to understand how we got to where we are and to break down the myths and stereotypes that run across the Asian American community. Asian Americans are too often a tokenized afterthought, getting pulled in when more diverse faces are needed.[1] Asian Americans are often perceived as successful due to the misconceived model minority myth.[2] On the whole, Asian Americans are sometimes classified on one hand as White and on the other hand as people of color. This complex set of conflicting stereotypes has rendered us invisible in America.[3]

Myth 1: Asian Americans are a single monolithic group

Asian Americans are not a monolith. They have a population of nearly 23 million, with a diverse group originating from more than 20 countries in East and Southeast Asia and the Indian subcontinent. They include many subgroups:

- East Asians: 4.9 million Chinese, 1.9 million Korean, 1.5 million Japanese, and 204 thousand Taiwanese;
- Southeast Asians: 4 million Filipino, 2.1 million Vietnamese, 322 thousand Cambodian, 313 thousand Thai, 309 thousand Hmong, 261 thousand Laotian, and 182 thousand Burmese;
- South Asians: 4.3 million Indian, 515 thousand Pakistani, 188 thousand Bangladeshi, and 168 thousand Nepalese;
- Pacific Islanders: 600 thousand Native Hawaiian, 209 thousand Samoan, 159 thousand Guamanian, and 253 thousand Other Pacific Islanders.

According to the US Census, the Asian American population is the fastest-growing racial or ethnic group in the United States, growing by 81 percent from 2000 to 2019.

Myth 2: Asian Americans are high earning and well educated

The income inequality in the United States is rising most rapidly among Asian Americans. Asian Americans displaced

Black Americans as the most economically divided racial or ethnic group in the United States, according to a Pew Research Center analysis of government data.[4] In fact,

- 12.3 percent of Asians live below the poverty line.[5]
- Asian Americans represented 17.9 percent of people living in poverty in New York City and had the highest poverty rate of any racial or ethnic group at 29 percent.
- Nearly 1.1 million Southeast Asian Americans are low-income, and about 460,000 live in poverty.[6]

Myth 3: Asian Americans are fairly represented in leadership positions

When it comes to Asian Americans in the workplace, most Asian Americans are hired at the bottom and not promoted to leadership roles. According to the Leading Asian Americans to Unite for Change 2021 STAATUS index report[7], nearly 50 percent of non–Asian Americans believe Asian Americans are fairly or overrepresented when in fact Asian Americans are significantly underrepresented in senior positions in companies, politics, and media. According to *DiversityInc*, Asian Americans make up only 2.6 percent of the corporate leadership of Fortune 500 companies.[8] Many Asian Americans face the challenge of not getting promoted in the workplace. For example, representation of Asian American talent is inconsistent across advertising agencies as reported by the Agency DEI Database, where Asians occupy only 13 percent professional, 6 percent management, 8 percent senior executive, and 5 percent c-suite roles. This is a snapshot of only one industry and an example of why we need change to ensure that Asians are recognized as leaders in the workplace.

Creating Visibility

Visibility is not only about the act of being seen by others. It is also about actively seeking opportunities to see ourselves. We are not asking you to change who you are but to create a framework of access and understanding. We believe that by keeping visibility at the forefront of your mind, you will be able to create opportunities for yourself and make sure your employers see you in the roles you desire.

Why did we choose the title *The Visibility Mindset?* Because Asian Americans are still an invisible minority, and to be visible you must keep an active mindset. In this book, we separate the visibility mindset into three parts: improving yourself, working with others, and redefining the future of the workplace.

Improving Yourself

This section provides strategies to improve yourself. You will discover how to nurture a lifelong learner mindset and how to activate a growth mindset in how you approach life. The Asian American community must unlock more opportunities by reframing their mindset and focusing their energy on self-improvement by shifting perspectives and reactions. The chapters in this section include topics on finding your voice, knowing your worth, building your personal brand, creating your own career path, finding your optimal work-life balance, and prioritizing your mental health.

Working with Others

This section covers stories of how we work with others throughout our career journeys and provides tips on how to navigate our career paths while learning from leaders who became successful by collaborating with others in the workplace. The chapters in this section include topics on addressing microaggressions, maximizing the power of networking, becoming an effective leader and manager, and optimizing the magic of mentorship.

Redefining the Future of the Workplace

We are writing this book as an essential career guide for you with the hope of improving the future of the workplace. We need to reimagine what our future looks like, and through our stories, we share how we can continue to reshape and improve the workplace to help Asian Americans thrive and flourish at work. The chapters in this section include topics on leveraging allyship and integrating diversity, equity, and inclusion into learning and development.

At the end of each chapter, reflections will help you to integrate the lessons from the chapter into your life to help get you to that job or position you've always imagined for yourself.

PART

I

Improving Yourself

1

Finding Your Own Voice

Bernice Chao

If people were silent, nothing would change.
—Malala Yousafzai, Pakistani activist for female education,
Nobel Peace Prize laureate

WHEN ASKED TO speak at the Omnicom Precision Marketing Group's (OPMG's) Asian Pacific Islander Collective, I was stunned that Van Tran, a principal at Credera, and Cathy Butler, the chief executive officer at Organic, had picked me to talk about charisma. As someone who constantly feels like a fish out of water no matter what room or conversation I am in, this would have never been a topic I would have chosen for myself. I discovered, however, that others see me as charismatic because of the strategies and techniques I consciously employ while speaking with others.

Learning how to communicate is vital for Asian Americans because they face a strong stereotype as technically competent, diligent, and quiet. Because of this perception, Asian

Americans are less likely to be promoted into management and leadership positions.[1] In western workplaces, those in leadership positions typically are praised for having qualities of being outgoing, bold, and sometimes even brash, which is at complete odds with how Asian Americans are seen in society.

A *New York Times* article reported that more than 160,000 student records showed that Harvard consistently rated Asian American applicants lower than others on traits such as "positive personality, likability, courage, kindness, and being widely respected."[2] This news was a painful reminder to Asian Americans of the ethnic stereotype that though they are hardworking, they are not perceived to possess communication skills.

Asian Americans must acknowledge the bias that exists and proactively combat it. It is not our responsibility to change society, but we can definitely challenge the stereotype of our individual performance by building charisma and developing interpersonal skills. As we collectively use our voices, we will start to reduce the stereotypes and redefine how we are perceived. This chapter will teach you how to find your voice and break the barriers that limit opportunities in the corporate world for Asian Americans.

Learning the Rules of Communication

To improve your social skills, it is essential to start where you are by acknowledging your personality traits and your communication style before you consider where you want your voice to be. No matter where you are in the process of learning communication skills in your professional career, you can always practice ways to improve and cultivate your voice. In other words, communication skills can be learned and refined whether you are an introvert or an extrovert. As an introvert, you may have traits that can benefit you such as being observational, a good listener, and more contemplative before speaking. As an extrovert, your skills can include being enthusiastic, extra friendly, and social.

Once you understand your personality traits, think about how you communicate through verbal and nonverbal cues. Having strong verbal and nonverbal communication skills demonstrates to your manager and leaders in your workplace that you can bring out the best in others, which is essential for career advancement and promotion into leadership positions.

Dr. Albert Mehrabian, a psychology professor at the University of California, Los Angeles, published the book *Silent Messages*, in which he discusses the 7-38-55 communication rule: 7 percent of meaning is communicated through the spoken word, 38 percent of meaning is communicated through tone of voice, and 55 percent of meaning is communicated through body language. This means that 93 percent of how you communicate comes from nonverbal communications, which you can refine and practice.

Recognizing the Steps to Effective Communication

Interpersonal skills or soft skills are the behaviors and tactics a person uses to interact with others effectively. Communication skills are crucial in your personal life and essential in your work life. Interpersonal skills seem to come naturally to some people, but even if they don't come naturally to you, you are capable of learning these skills with practice.

Having effective interpersonal skills helps build trust and collaboration between team members and managers.

The steps to effective communication include knowing your audience, practicing active listening, improving verbal communication, focusing on nonverbal communication, and asking for feedback.

Knowing Your Audience

In my experience as an Asian American in a White male–dominated career, I quickly realized I did not have the same cultural reference points as my colleagues. I didn't have the same music, sports, or movie knowledge because in my household my immigrant parents didn't expose me to those things at a young age. Any references I had, came after I went to college and started forming my own interests. Consequently, I often was unable to recall famous names of songs, quotes, or sporting event outcomes, which many of my colleagues used in peer-to-peer conversation. I had to adapt and learn ways around that by finding other reference points that I could expound upon to find commonality.

According to Drake Baer in his *Business Insider* article "If You Want to Get Hired, Act Like Your Potential Boss," managers hire and promote people based on people who remind them of themselves. If you want to work at a consultancy, law firm, bank, or elsewhere in the professional elite, landing a job may not require you to be the best qualified. Instead, it could depend on whether you have a "spark of commonality" with the hiring manager you interview with.[3]

In some American workplaces, knowing movie quotes and having an affinity for sports helps. However, if that's not in your interests, there are other ways to find commonality.

Strategy for Finding Commonality Before meeting with new individuals, spend 15 minutes before your meeting to learn what you can about them. Today, everyone has a digital footprint, whether on a company's website, personal website, LinkedIn, or social media sites. Look for natural ties and make a note of them. Look for organic ways that you can weave commonalities into your conversation. For example, did you live in a familiar place? Go to the same college? Have similar interests? Have mutual friends on LinkedIn?

I find this tactic especially important when interviewing; most interviewers see multiple candidates between their busy meetings, so finding ways to be memorable is essential. Finding common ground is an excellent way to keep the person on the other end of the conversation interested in engaging with you and staying top of mind. After an interview, you can reiterate these commonalities in your follow-up thank you email, which I send the same day as the interview because often your interviewee is asked to give feedback the same day.

Practicing Active Listening

As an Asian person, I was taught to have the answers to questions immediately ready so I would be seen as knowledgeable. I started to develop a bad habit of not listening to the speaker's full thoughts, and instead I would start forming the answer or the next question that I was going to give while the speaker was still talking. This came off as if I wasn't fully giving the speaker my full attention—mainly because I wasn't. I was too busy in my own head thinking about what to say next.

There are four steps to active listening: (1) focus, (2) reflect, (3) clarify, and (4) communicate.

Focus   Active listening requires that you go into a conversation focusing on listening to the speaker. You're giving the people you interact with your full attention and suspending judgment by not interrupting. You should close your computer or put away the phone, look the speaker in the eye, and focus on what they're saying and not on what you're going to contribute after they stop talking. For virtual conversations, it will help to look at a designated area on the screen so as not to seem distracted. You can self-regulate interruptions by muting yourself while the other person is speaking.

Reflect   Reflective listening deepens the emotions behind the message, and then offers them back to the speaker to confirm what has been said in your own words. Mirroring back key points of the conversation indicates that you were listening.

Common reflective stems:

"So you feel . . ."
"It sounds like you . . ."
"What I hear you saying . . ."
"I think I hear you saying . . ."
"I'm not sure if I follow, but I believe you're saying . . ."

Clarify   Clarifying is checking the understanding of the message by asking what was said to be repeated or by asking additional questions. This allows the speaker to go into detail and clarify what was said and allows the listener to remove doubt and check the accuracy of their understanding.

Common clarifying stems:

"Could you repeat . . . ?"
"I don't feel clear about . . ."

"When you said . . . , what did you mean?"
"When did this happen?"
"Can you further explain . . . ?"

Communicate After taking time to fully interpret the information given to you, you can respond by introducing your own ideas, experiences, and suggestions. Perhaps you can describe a similar experience you had or talk about an experience that was triggered by the conversation. Having a well-crafted response will show the speaker that you respect the time they're providing you and that you value the interaction.

> **Example:** *"I really appreciate you sharing about how you dealt with a manager giving you a hard time about a project in the workplace. It was helpful to hear you were able to use facts to defend yourself. I'm currently going through something similar where my manager was unexpectedly harsh, and I was able to speak with the head of human resources who helped as an impartial judge of the situation."*

Improving Verbal Communication

As an Asian woman of small stature, I have found that I really must make up for my smaller presence in my verbal delivery. I found early on in my career that when I contributed ideas in meetings, I was told that they were "cute"—mind you, these were not ideas about cute things. It was the managers in the room basing their response on how they perceived who I was by how I was conveying what I was saying. My voice was quiet, and I was speaking quickly and nervously. I found that to be taken seriously I had to make an effort to deliver the ideas I brought forward with authority.

I practiced making sure that I delivered my ideas as if everyone in the room were peers that I felt comfortable with and made sure I spoke at a good volume and pace and that I had conviction. I found that if I brought in supporting statements or statistics as to why my idea would be successful, I would be perceived with more authority and my idea would be met with more acceptance.

How you use your voice when you speak adds another layer of meaning to what you are saying. As you present, it is critical for you to explain the context to the audience for them to understand the logic behind your message to ensure it does not get misunderstood.

When it comes to verbal communication, here are some best practices to consider the next time you speak:

- **Pace the speed of your words:** Talking too fast may signal that you're not confident in the information you're delivering, or it may make the information being spoken unintelligible. Take your time when delivering your message.
- **Avoid filler words:** Be intentional to not use filler words such as *like, um, uh, okay, right, so,* and *you know.*
- **Be clear and concise:** It is not always necessary to share all the details of what is happening. You will be more effective when you are deliberate with your words and get straight to the point in a way your audience can easily comprehend.

A way to alleviate many communication problems is to make a conscious effort to breathe between sentences or topics and to recognize the power of pausing when you are speaking. Pausing helps your audience understand you better and enables you to gather your own thoughts as you are speaking.

Focusing on Nonverbal Communication

Your nonverbal communication is just as important as your verbal communication because it can determine whether a person has a positive or negative impression of you. Pay attention to your body language, and be conscious of the signals that your body is giving off during your conversation. You can show interest in a conversation by facing the speaker, talking, nodding along, and smiling. Light, enthusiastic hand gestures can accompany your responses. However, if the discussion is more serious, avoid smiling during the conversation. The same advice holds true in group settings: make sure you direct your gaze and body toward the person speaking in the room as the conversation moves from person to person.

As you recently learned, 38 percent of meaning in communication comes from tone. Your tone of voice is a major contributor to how your message is delivered to your audience. Communicating passionately, quietly, or angrily can affect how people interpret you. Your tone should sound firm but not harsh or unfriendly. You want to avoid a tone that is too soft or hard to be heard by everyone in the room.

Be mindful of your energy level as well. Enthusiasm for your project can make the listener more interested. However, if you are anxious, your anxiety may cause your listener to be uneasy; if your voice is monotone, the listener could lose interest and tune out.

You can practice your nonverbal communication skills, trying to achieve the outcomes shown in the table below.

Nonverbal Communication	Desired Outcome
Eye contact	Natural and relaxed with a soft gaze and few blinks
Tone	Calm, controlled, and even
Facial gestures	Nodding along with a relaxed jaw and relaxed smile
Body gestures	Good posture, hand, and arm movements while facing the speaker

You can easily show that you are disengaged or disapproving if your arms are folded across your body or you are sitting slouched with your legs pointing away from the speaker. You can even appear unconfident or untrustworthy if you are looking at the ground while someone is talking to you.

A technique known as *mirroring*, in which you mimic or copy your speaker's body language, has been proven to build trust subconsciously. In an article in *Forbes* magazine, "The Art and Science of Mirroring," Carol Kinsey Gorman talks about using mirroring in a business setting. She concludes that you will know that you have developed mutual rapport when your partner begins to mirror you in return. Change your arm position and see if she will match your movement into the new posture. If you were to use this technique in a sales presentation, and your prospect subconsciously matched your body language, you could take that as a signal of trust and rapport. But if your prospect mismatched you, you should consider the possibility that you have not yet persuaded her to your point of view. Consciously mirroring the speaker is an easy way to build subconscious familiarity.[4]

Asking for Feedback

The key way to improve how you utilize your voice is to ask for feedback. Feedback will help you learn how to make adjustments and make better progress in how you communicate. After a meeting, you can ask managers or peers who were in the meeting how they felt you performed. Did you appear confident, knowledgeable, and well prepared? What are some areas you can improve upon for the next meeting? Make an effort to keep practicing the skills that need work. Keep track of the feedback you receive to see whether your performance improves over time.

Improving Your Voice by Practicing

I remember early in my career being in a large conference room where we brainstormed the next Super Bowl commercial idea. There were high-level executives in the room, including the chief creative officer of the company. I felt too junior and was afraid to say something stupid and risk embarrassing myself. What happened was something worse: I spent a whole meeting without saying a word, and it looked like I didn't have a reason to be in the room in the first place.

By contrast, my peers in the room were shouting out random thoughts that came into their heads. Some ideas were good, many were terrible, but they were actively engaging. The meeting was a moment where I could have shown my prowess for thinking in front of high-level executives, but my fear of failure prevented me from doing so. Because I did not show any purpose for being in the room, I was not invited to the next meeting.

The lesson that I'm sharing with you is to speak up because you don't want to come off as wasted space. *You don't have to have the perfect answer to contribute.* Your idea may not be fully formed, but it could be the source of your team's breakthrough, and what you bring could help spark something for the rest of the group. Take advantage of every opportunity with an audience to be visible and heard.

Navigating Group Dynamics

Have you ever gone through a whole meeting without speaking or have you been afraid that if you said something half-baked, your response would reflect poorly on you? As you can see from my experience in the Super Bowl example, you are not alone.

Group communication is the act of being able to communicate with multiple members of a group at the same time. These group conversations are opportunities for individuals to come together to collaborate, discuss individual responsibilities, navigate setbacks, and so on. When many people are gathering, you have the opportunity to build credibility within the organization by showing you are an active participant in high-visibility discussions.

Prepare in Advance   To help you get ready for group meetings, take fifteen minutes before the meeting to prepare, check to see who is attending the meeting, review the agenda, and read through all materials. Consider having some possible questions and comments in advance, before the meeting. If you are engaging in virtual meetings, you can have these prepared on Post-its stuck around your screen as a reminder to engage.

Make it a point to speak up in every meeting that you're in with an original idea or opinion so that everyone in the room realizes why you were invited to the space in the first place. If this is uncomfortable for you, slowly build up the confidence to speak little by little. If this is still uncomfortable, you can send your ideas by email. You can also show that you're engaged with nonverbal cues, such as nodding along or giving a thumbs up.

Arrive Early When you show up late for something, people may assume that you are disorganized and kind of flakey. Showing up early can show your willingness to engage. According to Lifehacker, if you want to make a good impression, there's one simple thing you can do that makes a huge difference: show up to every commitment five minutes early.[5] When you show up late, you are disrupting the meeting; the meeting may need to start over, or people in the room may need to wait for you to get there. You could be missing key points or small talk of team members getting acquainted. Arriving late creates unnecessary anxiety all around.

Manage Conflict If someone in the group is sharing something contradictory or conflict-ridden, support that person's right to be heard. Think about how you would want to be treated if someone were to disagree with an idea you had; you would want to be supported and not be embarrassed. Remember you are on the same team and working toward the same goal. You can respond with any facts, data, or evidence to support that person's viewpoint or your own if it differs; you could still be in disagreement, but everyone's points would be heard.

Expand on Ideas   If the comment or question you were going to share has already been shared by someone else in the room, you can support the other person's idea and add on something like this: "Lu's idea was really great; here are ways we can bring it to life: . . ." This is also a great way to help other members be heard in the group, especially for those who are quieter, with a smaller presence. It shows that you're a great team player and that you validate others' ideas.

Engaging in Speaking Opportunities

I realized early on into my career that speaking parts were given to those in the room who were not the minorities. As someone who was seen as "that quiet Asian woman," I really had to assert myself as someone competent and up to the task. I eased in slowly by presenting a few pages of a deck (a slide presentation) internally, and then I gradually worked up the confidence to give external presentations to the client.

The first couple of presentations I was a ball of nerves, and while I still get nervous today, I'm able to prepare myself well enough to deliver messages confidently. I share on my personal website and on my LinkedIn that I have done speaking engagements so that I can break preconceived assumptions.

Another way to extend your voice and level of expertise in your field is by volunteering for various speaking roles at work. Being able to deliver knowledge to a room or on a public stage helps build credibility and broader recognition inside and outside the workplace.

Here are some ways to prepare for presentations and public engagements.

Rehearse Out Loud   Rehearse as much as possible. If feasible, do run-throughs in the room you would be presenting in to feel comfortable with the space. The more you practice, the more at ease you will be, and that confidence will come through in your delivery. Leading vocal awareness coach Arthur Samuel Joseph recommends watching yourself by practicing in a mirror and then recording yourself on a video or an audio recorder.

As you replay the audio, take notice of your tone and check whether the delivery is consistent with the content being presented.

Use Your Own Words   When practicing out loud, make sure that what you're saying sounds authentic and natural to you. It helps to create bullets for key points versus reading from a script. Do not overload presentation slides with too many words and then read from them. This can cause your presentation to drag and your viewers to disengage.

Find the Flow   Think about presentations as an event, where you want to make your viewers have a good experience as soon as they enter the room and until they leave it. Practice a captivating line to get your audience's attention. Structure your presentation so that your ideas have the most impact. For example, in advertising, it's common for us to present three campaign ideas, in this order:

1. Second-Place Idea	2. Third-Place Idea	3. First-Place Idea

The second-place idea is usually the idea that best represents the assignment and is the safest approach. This shows the client that you understood the ask right out of the gate. The third-place idea is buried in the middle deck. And finally, you place your best idea at the end, to finish the presentation on your most substantial and memorable piece.

Manage Time   In your run-through, it's good to make sure that you have adequate information to fill up the time but not so much that you can't get through all the work. Another reason to manage your time is that you want to make sure you don't take over someone else's speaking time. Also, you may need to leave some time for discussion at the end. A good practice is to note ahead of time how long you will spend on each portion of your presentation and make sure you can adapt on the go.

Considering Your Written Communication

It's not always about speaking up when it comes to finding your voice. Written communication is another way to leverage your unique perspective. Consider how you can improve your written communication as you keep working on sharing your perspective and putting your words into your thoughts.

Below are examples for how you can shape your voice through written communication.

Blog Posts   Sharing your point of view in an article or blog post is a great way to start working on building your voice. It creates space for you to share your expertise or experience on a topic you are interested in.

Emails   When writing emails, be clear and concise in a way appropriate to your audience. Emails are a great way to voice your opinion if it is easier for you to write rather than speak, at least in the short term. Try to practice different ways to exercise your voice; it will become stronger in time once you build more confidence from practicing.

Social Media   Be more intentional about knowing your worth and owning your story. You can practice writing about your career journey on social media. For example, LinkedIn is an excellent career tool where you can celebrate your accomplishments. You will learn more about this in future chapters.

Creating Safe Spaces to Speak Up

As the only Asian or only woman in most meetings, I found that expanding on other people's contributions made for a better team environment. This was a good way for me to help give other voices more support for what they said, especially people from marginalized communities. My approach as an ally helped them feel more comfortable being in the room to be seen and heard.

Make sure you are creating a safe space for representation at the table, which welcomes people to jump into conversations. As a leader, it is your responsibility to lead by example; others will follow you simply from you creating space for them. Invite people around you in the workplace to speak up; if they say something, they will feel valued when you make them realize they're there for a reason and not because of who they are and what they look like. It is critical to remind people that their viewpoint is not only unique and valuable but also welcomed in order to make the work better.

Interview with Scott Asai

Scott Asai is a professional speaker who specializes in teaching soft skills. He focuses on educating managers in communication, leadership, and emotional intelligence. Scott's brief, conversational, and practical style makes it easy for audiences to implement his suggested strategies. He has a bachelor's degree in psychology from Loyola Marymount University and a master's degree in organizational leadership from Biola University. He is a certified professional coach (iPEC Coaching), a certified strengths coach (Clifton Strengths), and a TEDx speaker ("Saving Soft Skills from Extinction"). In his free time, Scott enjoys spending time with his wife and two kids.

What do soft skills mean to you?

Soft skills are the ability to interact well with others. If you get hired because of hard skills, you get promoted because of soft skills. In the past few years, working virtually, the need for soft skills has only increased due to miscommunication/lack of connection happening more frequently online. Technology can diminish your soft skills simply because of convenience. Therefore, it's crucial to practice soft skills such as public speaking, leadership, and emotional intelligence, or else they will erode. With the addition of AI [artificial intelligence] and robots to the workforce, soft skills have become the differentiator from automation. I can't think of a more exciting time to improve your soft skills since they are becoming more valuable by the second!

Can you tell us a story of when your soft skills helped you?

About five years ago, I managed a team of 30 people remotely, primarily via Zoom. Fast-forward, who knew that experience would equip me for now? When communicating virtually, try to use the same principles that work in person: build trust, promote community, and develop people. Using active listening and empathy, I built rapport with my team quickly. I was utilizing tools like Slack. It took our work challenges to a more collaborative forum to brainstorm solutions together. Lastly, as a leader, I tried to understand the strengths of each team member so I could place them in roles and situations that allowed them to thrive. To me, soft skills are fueled by genuinely caring about people. If you lead with your heart first, you can figure out the skills/tactics later.

What presentation tips do you recommend?

Since we live in a virtual workplace, presenting videos is a new skill to master. Look directly into the camera while speaking as much as possible to show you're focused. Be sure to show emotion, as it captivates your audience to pay attention. Most importantly, keep your energy level high throughout the entire presentation. We've all experienced Zoom fatigue, but enthusiasm and passion from the presenter can be more impactful than even the content itself since it screams through the screen. Treat presenting virtually the same way you would treat public speaking. The only way to get over your fear of speaking in front of a crowd is to volunteer for opportunities to face them head-on. As someone who feared public speaking more than a decade ago, believe me when I say with practice, you will improve.

How has being an Asian American affected your career?

I've taken perceived disadvantages such as age, lack of experience, and setbacks to motivate me to prove what I can do.

Key Takeaways

- Everyone has an opportunity to learn communication skills, whether you are an introvert or an extrovert.
- Seven percent of meaning is communicated through the spoken word, 38 percent through tone of voice, and 55 percent through body language.
- Improve your interpersonal skills by combining preparation, active listening, vocal delivery, and body language.
- Group dynamics is essential for more visibility in the workplace and can be navigated by preparing, arriving early, mastering conflict resolution skills, and learning how to expand on others' ideas.
- Presentations are the best way to show that you have authority with your voice. Ways to refine this skill are to rehearse, use your own words, find the flow, manage time, and find extra coaching.

Reflections

- Take the "Are You an Introvert or Extrovert?" quiz available at https://susancain.net/quiet-quiz.
  - o If you are an introvert, try to speak up at least 1–2 times in your next meeting.
  - o If you are an extrovert, try to create space for others by allowing other meeting attendees to share their voice.
- Are you communicating in the most effective way, based on the topic?
  - o This chapter provides a tone of voice reflection chart for you to assess whether you're using the right tone for your presentation.
- What is your body language saying?
  - o Watch this TED talk by Amy Cuddy, "Your Body Language May Shape Who You Are," and consider what your body language is saying. https://bit.ly/body-langauge-amy-cuddy.
- Work on improving your presentation skills. The following are good resources to help you on this journey:
  - o Toastmasters;
  - o Shine Bootcamp;
  - o Agora Speakers;
  - o Masterclass.

2

Knowing Your Worth

Jessalin Lam

Self-worth is how you value yourself. It's not based on what others think of you or the things you have or haven't accomplished—it comes from within. But it's easy to forget that our worth isn't determined by outside forces.
—Stephanie Jade Wong, writer and editor

SELF-WORTH IS AN internal measure of how you value yourself and how you trust your own judgment in making decisions. The concept of self-worth was not introduced to me until my adulthood, and I now know the importance and benefits a focus on self-worth has throughout life.

This chapter will teach you the importance of self-worth and provide you with tips and examples for how to leverage it to benefit yourself in the workplace—from negotiating your salary to asking for a promotion and more. Typically in Asian culture, we are not taught to ask for more, and we embrace the freedom of silence. We do not think verbalizing everything is necessary. But to be successful in the western workplace, Asians must unlearn some of the cultural beliefs they have been taught throughout their lives and learn to embrace their self-worth.

Understanding What Self-Worth Is Not

To understand what we mean by self-worth, let's discuss some negative examples that do *not* define your self-worth:

- Your performance review;
- Your job title;
- Your financial status and salary.

Asians are often known to value hard work and career success and focus too much on achievements. However, a score on a performance review will never define your worth and the value you bring. Do not evaluate yourself based on what an employer may say about you when you are doing your best. Instead, reframe how you are perceiving feedback to navigate the areas that you may want to improve.

Your job title also is not who you are. When we are in a professional setting or networking situation, we are often asked what our profession is and feel judged by a mere job title. Remember that a title is only a name. Of course, we want to elevate Asians to break the bamboo ceiling for those who want to climb the corporate ladder to executive positions in corporate America. However, do not get caught up in solely the job title. Focus more on what you are learning and doing that will take you to the next level in your career.

Similarly, financial status is often overrated. No dollar amount should equate to the value you place on yourself. Your self-worth should be independent of your financial status and pay.

When it comes to self-esteem, Asians have been reported to have the lowest self-esteem compared to other races/ethnicities.[1] Why might that be? One of the factors that influences low self-esteem among Asian Americans is how they have been raised by their parents. For example, 39 percent of Asian Americans say that their parents from their country of origin subgroup put too much pressure on their children to do well in school.[2] If you are pressured to do well, you aim for perfection and are unconsciously taught that you may not be good enough. In Asian culture, we generally are not taught about self-worth growing up; we are told that self-esteem is supposed to be earned rather than it being considered a right.

Overcoming Imposter Syndrome

A huge obstacle that relates to your self-worth is imposter syndrome, which is defined as doubting your abilities and feeling like a fraud. It is a pattern of self-doubt that leads to anxiety, stress, and missed opportunities. Asian Americans, in particular, experience much higher rates of impostor feelings than their peers. The combination of academic stereotypes, parental expectations, and minority status all contribute to these feelings of being inadequate and a fraud. Asian Americans face high cultural expectations of achievement from their parents and "model minority" expectations from their peers—given these pressures, it's not surprising that they feel insecure about their status.[3]

When imposter syndrome kicks in, take a moment to address why you feel like an impostor and remind yourself why you're not an impostor. An Impostor Syndrome Actualization Chart is a good tool to get some self-reaffirming advice for yourself. In the table that follows, use the first column to state in what areas you feel like a fraud. For example, "I'm not good enough at <u>public speaking</u>," "I don't deserve _____," "I can't _____," or "I don't belong in _____." In the second column, write all the reasons why you do actually have skills and are not a fraud. This is your contradictory support, which refutes the statements in the first column. For example, "Last week, I gave a talk to my co-workers about the latest sales numbers, and it went well." This chart is a helpful way to track your success and build confidence in your abilities.

Ways You Feel Like a Fraud	Contradictory Support

Knowing the Value You Bring to Work

We can now move on to examples of healthy self-worth that can help you in your own life. First, let's talk about the high value you bring to the world. Take a pause from this book and think about what makes you uniquely valuable in your current role or where you would like to be.

Reflecting on Your Unique Value

Here are some starter questions to kick off your brainstorming:

- What knowledge and skills do you bring to the workplace?
- Do you carry a level of empathy as a leader to your team?

- Do you have skills that help your organization be more efficient in ways of working?
- Do you honor your words and commitment to be reliable?
- Are you a lifelong learner, constantly learning, unlearning, and relearning to do better?
- Consider your entire work experience. Does this invite you to bring transferable skills to your current role that others would not have?

How did that feel, to evaluate yourself? It is often a difficult exercise for many of us, and it is important to take the time to self-reflect and be intentional with how you speak to yourself. Believe in yourself, and do not doubt your ability to do your job.

Amplifying What You Bring to the Table

Here are some things to consider when thinking about the value you bring to the workplace:

- **Reframing your mindset:** How you speak to yourself has a bigger impact than you think. You have the power to retrain your brain to perceive yourself the way you want. Make a list of your strengths and how you solve challenges to reframe your mind as a proactive problem solver. This will remind you how you have self-control of your thoughts, actions, and reactions in life.
- **Adding value:** Think about how to add value to the workplace by the business results you are creating. Consider the bottom line and big picture of your role and how you fit into the larger puzzle of the business. For example, are you bringing in new business, saving the organization money, or adding value in other ways?
- **Trusting yourself:** People often doubt themselves, especially when facing the unknown. You need to trust

that you are doing the best with what you have. Believe in yourself and know that you are capable of anything you put your mind to.

Advocating for Yourself

When it comes to your self-worth, be your own best friend. Be your own best advocate and cheerleader to celebrate your accomplishments for all that you have done with your life to be who you are today. In the previous chapter, you learned about finding your voice and using it to advocate for yourself. Now that you know your worth, take the time to pause and celebrate your wins. The more you celebrate the small and big wins in your life, the more of them you will attract. When you celebrate your accomplishments, endorphins are released inside your body, reinforcing the desire for you to want to keep showing up in this way for yourself.

Negotiating Your Salary

When thinking about negotiating their salary, many people are intimidated or may not know where to start. Learn how to have these conversations sooner rather than later to reap the benefits. When I was talking to a recruiter for my first six-figures job, it was scary to not know what to say or how to tackle the conversation. Fortunately, I had a friend who prepared me on what to expect and how to say the right words for the next steps. When I heard the first verbal offer, I wanted to say yes because it was significantly higher than my current salary. But I had been underpaid most of my career, and I channeled my inner voice to stay calm and listen to my friend's advice on staying confident to ask for more. I was able to ask for 25 percent more salary and more paid time off to be included in my compensation package. I let them know if they offered that to me, I would be able to sign the offer letter that same week. I also let them know how much I appreciated their consideration.

My experience is only one example of negotiating a salary. I encourage you to know your fair market value and do your research ahead of time to set yourself up for success. Some of the resources to find your fair market value include Glassdoor, Simply Hired, LinkedIn, Payscale, and Salary.com.

Statistics have shown that Asian American women make only $0.93 to the white man's dollar, and Native Hawaiian and other Pacific Islander women make $0.79 to the white man's dollar.[4] We need to change this by starting to ask for more when negotiating salary. To begin, we must know what others are getting paid. Typically, Asians may not be comfortable talking to each other about how much money they make, unlike their white colleagues. This difference puts Asian Americans at a disadvantage. Asian Americans must start asking people how much they make and get comfortable talking about money to ensure they are getting paid their worth.

Other negotiations may center on severance packages. For example, an Asian friend who was laid off due to company restructuring consulted people in her network and a labor lawyer in order to understand what the standard best practices were in order to negotiate a better package. Asians may often accept what is given to them, be grateful and move along, but they are often short-changed. In these situations, make sure you do your homework to know what is negotiable.

When negotiating salary, don't only think about the money your employer is paying you. Consider the entire compensation package, which could include the following:

- **Paid days off:** Employers may give a specified number of days off or may offer unlimited paid time off.
- **Flexible work schedule:** Employers may offer flexibility to work from home or allow the employee to create a schedule that best suits their current life situation.
- **Severance package:** Some employers offer pay and benefits to an employee upon termination or completion of their employment.
- **Bonus structure:** Employee incentive programs may be offered beyond an employee's salary based on metrics being met.
- **Employer contribution to health insurance:** Some companies may offer to pay for some percentage of an employee's health insurance.
- **Education and training opportunities:** Employers could pay for a portion of an employee's education if they decide to go back to school for an additional degree or provide a professional development stipend to employees to invest in their growth.
- **Parental leave:** Some companies offer paid time off to both parents after the birth or adoption of a child.
- **Dependent care:** Some companies offer paid time off to take care of an elderly or sick person.
- **Relocation opportunities:** Some employers allow employees to relocate to another office location and could offer relocation expenses if needed.

All of these benefits are potentially negotiable.

Knowing When to Leave

Sometimes a work environment is so toxic that you should leave it. Knowing when to leave can be challenging.

To share my personal experience, I have been underpaid most of my life, and I have finally learned to be paid what I deserve thanks to people in my network, books, resources, and communities such as Ladies Get Paid. I've been in work environments where they have laid off everyone on the team except me, and when I asked for a raise, the employer said they didn't have the budget for it. A few months later, they hired someone white for a higher salary! Immediately afterward, I started looking for a new job knowing that I deserved to be treated better.

Unfortunately, many employers will take advantage of their workers and treat them like a robot or number rather than a human being with unique skill sets and experiences. It is critical for you to remember that your self-worth is more important than you can imagine. Don't let anyone tell you that you're not worth it, because you are. You should leave any employer who does not appreciate you. Here are some of the signs to know that it is time to leave an employer:

- You do not respect your boss.
- You are not being provided growth opportunities to learn and gain new skills.
- Your promotion was delayed after the employer mentioned they are working on it.
- No support or resources are given for an additional workload.
- The work culture is toxic, and you are not proud of working there.
- The company has high turnover, with people constantly leaving.
- The job has long work hours with low pay.

Interview with Clara Luo

Clara Luo is a first-generation Chinese American navigating the corporate world as a marketing leader and growth strategist. Her nonlinear career path spanned industries from financial services, consulting, advertising, and marketing. Over the past decade, she has been focused on defining strategic growth road maps for brands, companies, and people. Clara is dedicated to helping others find their path to growth. She lectures at various universities on all things related to brand and cultural disruption. She graduated from the Questrom School of Business at Boston University with a Bachelor of Science in business administration with a dual concentration in finance and marketing.

Can you share what "know your worth" means to you?

We often equate "know your worth" with focusing on external validations, like title, salary, equity, etc. Before you go through the action of negotiating—it all begins with understanding who YOU are, what you bring to the table, and placing value on your future self. For me, I learned about knowing your worth when I negotiated for a higher hourly rate as a lifeguard at 15 years old. I felt incredibly accomplished and learned that getting paid more is more than asking for what you want—it's about the act of fiercely defending what you're worth and what you want.

In the workplace, how have you leveraged your self-worth to your advantage to create opportunities for yourself?

Since I've learned to know my self-worth, I constantly educate myself by attending a lot of conferences or

workshops, reading self-help books, and practicing negotiating salaries especially when accepting new job offers.
This is easier said than done of course, especially as we
continue to go higher in our careers and the negotiations
become more complicated and multifaceted with new
variables in the mix. Often for women, people of color,
first generation, immigrants—anyone who comes from an
underrepresented group—we often are so grateful to just
have a job or be there, we convince ourselves that we have
enough. This is where I have leveraged my self-worth for
more opportunities by negotiating my salary and compensation packages throughout my career along with
transitioning my career into a different industry from
finance to marketing/advertising.

**What are the best ways people could ask for a promotion
and what do you advise them to include in their pitch?**
We focus a lot of conversations these days about asking
for promotions, but we don't spend enough time around
how to articulate the ask. It is generally harder for
minorities to get raises and promotions, so it's important
for people of color to practice articulating how to ask for
a promotion. For your promotion pitch, key questions to
consider in your ask include:
1. What is the vision of your job at this new level? What
   new perspectives will you bring to the table? Why are
   you worth more now?
2. What have you accomplished so far? Have you gone
   above and beyond to demonstrate you are performing
   at the next level? Have you taken or asked for stretch
   projects? Have you proven a positive business impact
   for your boss, your team, and your department?

3. How are your relationships with your stakeholders (i.e., clients, your boss, your colleagues, your peers)? Who is willing to go to bat for you? Do you have enough people who are willing to say your name and vouch for you when you're not in the room?

What advice would you share with our community related to getting what you are worth in terms of money?

It is about understanding your value, what you've brought to the table, how you've helped others, and most importantly your future value. It's important to not only ask for more but also learn how to articulate the ask so that it resonates with your manager. Sometimes we think because we've worked hard, we will deserve it, but that's only half the battle. What's important is that we have worked hard, added value and also created value for other people in the company, who will then vouch for you.

How has being Asian American affected your career?

Being a Chinese American woman has had a greater profound impact on others around me than on myself. Had you asked me this question over a decade ago, I think my perspective would have been different. By being a minority and a child of immigrant parents, I have valuable and diverse perspectives that I bring to the workplace. It's made me better at my craft, better at understanding others, having empathy, and noticing patterns that may not be obvious to a majority. We can choose to focus on the negatives, or shift the narrative to the positives—my identity has very much leaned into who I am. After all, I am who I am, and I have continued to bring forth my value and my perspectives to the table.

Key Takeaways

- It is up to you to design the life you want to live; do not settle for less.
- Change the narrative and know that you are enough, you are worthy, and you are valuable.
- Asian Americans experience higher rates of imposter syndrome. This is why it is essential for you to practice being confident and putting forth what you're good at.
- Reflect on healthy examples of self-worth to understand your unique value, amplify what you bring to the table, and advocate for yourself.
- Don't be afraid to ask for what you want. Know your fair market value, and look at the whole compensation package, not only the base salary, when negotiating. Be sure to include other benefits.
- Know the red flags on when to leave an employer who does not appreciate you.

Reflections

- **Use the Imposter Syndrome Actualization Chart.**
  - This chapter provides a chart for you to assess why you feel like a fraud and to consider contradictory support.
- **What is your fair market value based on your job, industry, and location?**
  - Use sources like Ladies Get Paid, Payscale.com, Salary.com, and Glassdoor to set yourself up for success when negotiating your salary.
- **Track your success to celebrate.**
  - Record the value you bring to the workplace that includes the project, business results, and the impact you created toward the bottom line.

- **What is included in your compensation package?**
  - o Consider benefits that you can ask for including paid days off, flexible work schedule, severance, bonus, training opportunities, relocation, and more.

3

Building Your Personal Brand

Bernice Chao

You do not just wake up and become the butterfly. Growth is a process.

—Rupi Kaur, poet and author

WHEN IT COMES to your personal brand, it will take time to develop your own story for how you want people to perceive you. For us, the personal branding we built for Asians in Advertising, a community to elevate Asians into executive positions, led to a feature in *Forbes* and to Wiley Publishing to organically reach out to us to see if we would be interested in writing a book to support Asians in the workplace. This is a great example where you never know where your personal brand can lead you. This chapter will teach you the importance of understanding what makes you unique, building your personal brand in a more strategic way, and crafting your own story in an elevator pitch.

47

Asian Americans are generally taught to downplay achievements and be humble about them. However, bragging about yourself in the western workplace is vital in your professional life. It's important to talk about your achievements to gain credibility and visibility with your employer or clients. Asians are known to be collectivistic, value humility, and tend to make decisions based on the common good rather than personal gain. On the other hand, their White counterparts are known to be individualistic, self-promote by competing with peers, and make decisions based on personal ambition.[1] In other words, if you have two people of equal talent and one communicates their achievements better than the other during an interview, you can guess who will seem more qualified than the other. Asian Americans need to actively practice owning their story by communicating what they have accomplished based on real facts and results. As an Asian American, crafting your personal brand story will be an essential tool to advocate for yourself and the skills you possess.

Defining Your Personal Brand

Let's start with defining what a personal brand is to ensure you understand what we are talking about. The term refers to how you strategically think about the image you want to build and how it fits in with your career and life. Your personal brand should show off the unique skills and experiences that make up who you are and will set you apart from other people. When you think about your personal brand, it allows you to showcase your strengths to open new doors for yourself. Your personal brand will be what people talk about when you are not in the room that will lead to more opportunities including job interviews, speaking engagements, networking opportunities, promotions, and referrals.

A personal brand is the same concept as product branding, only the product you are marketing is yourself. This is your chance to show off and allow critical decision makers to see that you're a superstar.

Understanding What Makes You Unique

Murphy Perng is a sommelier and founder of Matter of Wine, an educational wine events service. When Murphy started her business, she had to identify what would make her business unique and realized there was a lack of private wine tasting events, and the ones she attended made wine unapproachable. Through her understanding of what was lacking in the wine events market, Murphy crafted her value proposition as "private sommelier services that specialize in fun and educational wine tasting."

To be able to separate yourself from everyone else, you need to have a unique value proposition that sets you apart from others, one that is not too generic. You want to be remembered and thought of when it comes to moments of big decisions, such as getting hired and getting promoted. This starts with understanding who you are and what makes you unique. Self-awareness is critical for you to acknowledge where you are today and where you want to be in the future for your own personal brand.

Knowing Your Strengths

When you know what you are good at, you can work on shining a light on your strengths while managing your weaknesses. Here is how you can start to identify the strengths that you can build into your personal brand:

1. **Identify what you think of as your strengths:** Consider what you have done in the past that was exceptional and make a strength list for yourself to reference. This knowledge of what you do better than most people will help lay out your unique value proposition.
2. **Ask your network:** An exercise that could help you discover your strengths is by asking 5–10 people in your personal and professional network to let you know what your strengths are in their perspective. This will help you increase your self-awareness of how others perceive you.
3. **Select the strengths to focus on:** Once you've identified your strengths, finalize the ones that make sense for you to move forward with that you want to tie into your personal brand.

Reflecting on Your Current Personal Brand

In addition to knowing your strengths, it is critical to know where your current personal brand stands. Your brand, whether you choose to create it or not, already exists. It's what people think of when they hear your name, what pops up on a Google search, and what your social media shows. Reflect on what people may be saying about you when you are not in the room. How people perceive you and the unique value you bring is your personal brand.

A test to see where your brand stands is to Google your full name, and if you have a common name, add in your city or your profession with your search term. This search term should pull up relevant sites that reaffirm your brand; if nothing shows up, then you haven't spent much time on your online presence. So imagine if your name was Googled and nothing came up, but your competition got Googled, and a bunch of stuff reaffirmed they're an expert in the field.

You do not have to worry if nothing shows up now, as we are here to remind you to start where you are and work on improving your personal brand with tips from this chapter. The next step is to think about what else you want to add into the mix of ingredients as you continue to build the recipe of your personal brand.

Learning How to Build a Strategic Personal Brand

Jerry Lee, the co-founder of Wonsulting, talks about how he created his brand by sharing his professional development journey on LinkedIn. He wrote about his first promotion, the mistakes he made, the rejections, and his parents' teachings. Eventually, Jerry became more vulnerable by talking about his personal experience of having student loans, growing up low income, and being first-generation. When he started sharing more about his personal experience, he saw a swift growth in audience and now has over a million followers across TikTok, LinkedIn, and Instagram.

Your personal brand needs to be authentic to who you are and what you like to do. Authenticity is important because developing a brand doesn't happen overnight; it may take years to build up credibility in a particular subject and continually craft your message and your digital presence to support it. To start, let's consider the steps you need to take to build your personal brand in a more strategic way.

Diving Deeper to Know Who You Are

Now that you've detected your strengths, let's dig deeper into who you are. It is essential to pause and reflect on what it is you're trying to accomplish on your career journey. Here are questions to ask yourself:

- What do I want to be known for?
- What are my values and what is important to me?
- What skills and traits are my strengths?
- What are my weaknesses?
- What kind of work excites me? What am I passionate about?
- What industries are the most interesting to me?
- Where do I want to end up in my career?
- What kind of impact do I want to have?

It's okay if your answers to these questions change over time because you and your brand will evolve. However, it is crucial to answer these questions honestly to hone in on what you want to include in your brand. Whether these questions are easy or hard, it's good to consult with friends, co-workers, and family members. It's great to get outside feedback because it's not always easy to see yourself, and it could give you insights on things you haven't considered. Understanding who you are will guide you toward what you want to focus on.

Crafting an Elevator Pitch

Once you have gathered your answers about your strengths and who you are, you can start to paint the bigger picture of your brand and the direction you want it to go. The great thing is that once you have a clear picture of who you are and what you offer, you will attract like-minded people to you, helping you gain the visibility you ultimately want.

The next step is to craft an elevator pitch, a quick summary of your background and experience, to get someone interested in what you're saying. The reason it's called an *elevator pitch* is that it should be short enough to communicate it to someone during a short elevator ride. Having a pitch ready can be great for networking, attending professional events, job interviews, and more.

A great way to start is to develop a four-step elevator pitch:

1. **Introduce yourself:** Start by introducing yourself to share who you are and what makes you unique for the listener to hear.
2. **Share what you do:** Include a summary of what you do along with your value proposition and supporting skills. Make sure to include your achievements and business impact in your pitch.
3. **Explain what you want:** Be clear about what you hope to achieve and include what you want from others.
4. **Close with a call to action:** Make sure you end with a call to action for the person to know what to do or how to react to your message—whether that is keeping in touch, scheduling a meeting, offering an interview, or sharing a recommendation.

Elevator Pitch Example: *Hi, my name is Matt, and I work as a certified public accountant. I am seeking a position that will allow me to use the skills and strengths I acquired as an employee for 8 years at Ernst & Young while working on top Fortune 500 companies. I am now looking to take my skills to an exciting new opportunity. I saw you posted a job opening at your company, and I would like to learn more about the position. Would you be willing to talk to me next week?*

For best practices, remember to keep it brief and captivating and no longer than 60 seconds. Your pitch may be adjusted based on who you're speaking to and should not include your entire résumé. The pitch needs to be an interesting positive conversation that's relevant to your listener.

Communicating Your Personal Brand

Once you are comfortable with the elevator pitch and story you crafted around your personal brand, it is time for you to start sharing this to the world, whether that is in written or verbal form. The more practice you get sharing your story, the better your pitch will become as you hone in and manifest it into your reality.

The following are some strategies for how you can practice refining your personal brand pitch:

- **Say it out loud:** When you're at a networking event, try to share your elevator pitch out loud and see how people react while also reflecting on how it feels to say it out loud.
- **Ask for feedback:** Once you have honed in on what you want your brand to focus on, ask people in your network what they think of your pitch to see if you are missing anything essential to add to your story.
- **Create a personal website:** For your digital presence, you can start with creating your own website that ultimately controls your narrative and personal brand. It should include your professional headshot, an "About You" description, a unique value proposition, examples of what you do, a résumé with accomplishments, links to social media, and testimonials.

■ **Utilize LinkedIn:** If you're a working professional, LinkedIn is an important career tool that can act as a more concise version of your website along with the connections to people who can create more opportunities for your career. Make sure your LinkedIn profile reflects your personal brand, including your headshot, engaging headline, "About Me" with your value proposition, relevant experience, and testimonials from connections. You can post a few times a week with your expertise and point of view related to your personal brand.

Focusing on the Positive Impact

If you are questioning why you are developing your personal brand, remind yourself of the outcome and the positive impact of your personal brand. As Michelle Phan of Em Cosmetics has said, "My quick tip on personal branding is to remember you are your brand, no matter what your current job is, what project you happen to be working on at any one time or whatever the priority happens to be today. . . . always keep in mind the impact you leave on others and remember all we have is our own reputation and that's our brand, so be awesome to each other!"[2] This is a great reminder to stay positive as we are here to help others—keep that in mind as you evolve your own brand.

Discovering Examples of Strong Personal Brands

To wrap up your learning, here are examples of strong personal brands from Asian leaders in our community. This is another way to learn by observing how others showcase their personal brand. Adopt what may work for you as you figure out how to pitch your own story.

- **David Shing ("Shingy"):** David Shing was hired as AOL's first and only "Digital Prophet." He worked there from 2007 to 2019. His title drew criticism when it was first announced in 2007 for what seemed like a fairly standard marketing role; however, this title cemented his expertise in technology, and years later he can be found giving leadership talks. The name "Shingy" is uniquely memorable and his one-of-a-kind job title makes him and his image a remarkable example of a carefully curated personal brand.
- **Cindy Gallop:** Cindy Gallop is the founder of "If We Ran the World" and "Make Love Not Porn." She's a leading advertising executive turned entrepreneur and has completely transformed the way we talk about sex, relationships, and self-representation in the twenty-first century. She has a signature look with her platinum blond bob and refers to herself as the "The Michael Bay of Business."
- **Steve Hiroyuki Aoki:** Steven Hiroyuki Aoki is a DJ and innovator who has created an image and name for himself that is immediately recognizable. His career has included being a record producer, music programmer, and record executive with the creation of his record label, Dim Mak Records. In 2012, Pollstar designated Aoki as the highest grossing electronic dance music artist in North America from tours. His brand transcends music as he has created products with his name or his likeness, including Pizzaoki.

Interview with Kevin Yu

Kevin Yu is the Founder and CEO of SideChef, an all-in-one cooking experience platform that uses tech innovation to guide consumers through a seamless cooking and grocery shopping process. Born and raised in Silicon Valley as a first-generation Asian American, Kevin is a serial tech entrepreneur who perpetually builds products for the future. With a background in the gaming industry, Kevin combined inspiration from a failed dinner date and a passion to transform the food industry to pioneer SideChef, a modern and approachable step-by-step platform for people to cook at home with audio and visual cues. To date, Kevin led SideChef to raise over $10 million in funding. Kevin is an industry innovator in the food tech space as well as a three-time TEDx speaker. He has been recognized in the Forbes Next 1000 list. He is dedicated to educating other entrepreneurs on best practices, creative thinking, and invention. Kevin holds a bachelor's degree from the University of Southern California.

What tips do you have for building a personal brand?

Personal branding starts by defining how you give meaning to your everyday actions, followed by identifying your "great elevator pitch," and then being able to say that over and over. Building a brand is about consistency. This consistency is important because in a world full of uncertainty, people gravitate toward things and ideas that can be unequivocally true and reliable.

What was the most important lesson for the elevator pitch?

Every good pitch can be narrowed to a single sentence. If you need more, it isn't concise enough. If your idea is an exception—well, it isn't. The importance of having it in a single sentence is both to be packaged perfectly for the listener to understand, remember, and potentially share it out to others.

The importance of having it in a single sentence for yourself is so you have focus and clarity on your objective and direction in achieving it. Anytime I've not been able to explain an idea or even a single meeting's objective in a single sentence, it has been a red flag to me that I needed to prepare further because the ideas have not been fully distilled, and every pitch and meeting can have the potential to be the next checkpoint to where you are headed.

How can you identify your personal strength?

Identifying personal strength is similar to connecting supply and demand—and that crossing is where the magic happens. Personal strength should be both what you are passionate and good at, as well as a contribution that can be recognized within your peer group or larger. The common Asian stereotype portraying a mismatch in this supply and demand in passion is, "My parents wanted me to become a doctor, so I studied to become one, and while now I'm a decent doctor, it turns out I hate being one." Similarly, there is a mismatch if your environment doesn't appreciate or support your strength. You can take the seed of the tallest tree in the world, but if you plant it in the desert, nothing will grow.

Over my career, I've come to realize one of my personal strengths is being able to lead very ordinary people to achieve extraordinary results, which I spent most of my life not understanding as a strength. As a self-professed introvert throughout my life, I never saw myself as the "classic" leader. I wasn't the smartest, or the fastest, or the most charismatic. I often found myself being a "leader" in groups that you would normally classify as "not the most influential" in their environments or the "rag-tag" team. For instance, in college, I played a game called World of Warcraft where I led a group of one hundred people, from teenagers to retirees, ranging from unemployed to working professionals, in a virtual world, to defeat virtual dragons and monsters. This is hardly a story about what you'd call a "real" leader's leader. Looking back—it didn't matter. I was passionate about leading people and worked with whomever to conjure a way for them all to work together to accomplish difficult challenges. It didn't matter that the people worked together virtually. It didn't matter that the accomplishments were virtual. Heck, it didn't matter that I had not met any of these people in real life. I had a passion for leading these people and they recognized my ability to do so.

Today, I run a high-growth start-up company, doing eight figures of revenue yearly, started from a "rag-tag" ordinary team, built from a three-bedroom apartment, that has been able to achieve some extraordinary results. Follow your passion. Continuously find ways to improve what you are good at. Surround yourself with people that recognize your abilities, whoever they are, and embrace your own unique story that may one day redefine what "leadership" or whatever your personal strength may look like.

How do you communicate your personal brand?

What you should be trying to do in most effectively communicating your personal brand, is to figure out both the *best medium* and *methodology* to connect your personal strength to your target environment. How you can best communicate your personal brand, whether it be through social channels, media, or even the voice or language you use such as "humble bragging" is important. Ask yourself these questions:

■ **What is my personal strength/personal brand?**
  o Reference those questions and answers.
■ **Who will best recognize my talents?**
  o If I'm an amazing athlete, maybe coaches or agents are the people I need to find.
■ **Where are these people?**
  o If they all live in Los Angeles, maybe I should consider moving there to develop my acting skills further.
■ **How do they get information?**
  o If they are all following #instafood on Instagram, maybe I should be posting a bunch of my talent food photography there.
■ **What voice will connect them with the best?**
  o If they are attracted to confidence, maybe I can show them my boldest voice first, before exposing them deeper into my core strengths.

Key Takeaways

■ Personal branding is about marketing yourself like you would a product.

- Bragging about yourself in the western workplace is vital. Asian Americans need to actively own their personal brand and curate their story to include their accomplishments.
- Self-awareness is critical to acknowledge where you are today and what makes you unique, setting you apart from others.
- The four-step elevator pitch includes introducing yourself, sharing what you do, explaining what you want, and closing with a call to action.
- Even if you don't want to create a personal brand for yourself, know that it will be created for you regardless, so it's better to facilitate your own narrative.

Reflections

- **What are your strengths that contribute to your personal brand?**
  - o Take a free strengths test to discover your strengths from sites including https://high5test.com and https://www.viacharacter.org.
  - o Ask 5–10 people in your network to share what they think your strengths are.
- **Assess your current personal brand.**
  - o Google search your name to see what shows up. This will give you a starting point as you work on your digital presence.
- **Dive deeper to know who you are.**
  - o Pick 10–15 values from a list of values that are most important to you https://brenebrown.com/resources/dare-to-lead-list-of-values.

4

Creating Your Own Career Path

Jessalin Lam

*Having a short- and long-term plan for your career path is crucial
as this is what will keep you focused. But it is just as important to
keep an open mind as various unexpected opportunities will appear
along your journey. And though they may not always seem like
a logical choice at first, take some time to reflect as you may be
surprised at what skills and knowledge you can transfer over into
a role or industry that you didn't previously consider.*
　　　　—Leo Wong, DEI (Diversity, Equity, and Inclusion)
　　　　　　　　　　　champion and adjunct professor

THIS CHAPTER WILL empower you to be a trailblazer of your
own career path. It will teach you how to take action and
understand when the right time is to make a leap to a new
job or a career pivot if you are looking for something
different. Know that you have the power to shift where you
are headed. We will also help guide you on a path to
becoming more visible in your professional life.

Being a Trailblazer

What does it mean to be a trailblazer? I was first called a trailblazer when I participated in the Advertising Club of New York's i'mPART Women Fellowship in 2018. This is an incredible year-long executive and leadership training program designed specifically for mid-level rising female stars in the industry. When I heard my mentor, Ericka Riggs, say that I was a trailblazer, I did not believe it myself until I started thinking about what a trailblazer is and what they do.

I googled the word *trailblazer* and wondered if this was really who I was. Essentially, a trailblazer is someone who is a lifelong learner and pioneer in any field as they create a path for others to follow into the unknown or a new way of navigating a journey that may not have existed before. It takes an innovative mind to be a trailblazer. Trailblazers are creating a better world for others by showing that it is possible to create new paths and having the confidence to make it happen even when they may not have all the answers. For me, my trailblazing was born out of necessity; it was needed to survive and advance in the business word. My experience makes clear that all of us can learn to become trailblazers.

Here are some tips on how to practice becoming a trailblazer to support you in creating your own path:

- Follow your heart in what you want to do;
- Have the courage to believe in yourself as you create your next steps;
- Do not compare your path to anyone else's;
- Reflect on how far you've come, and keep going toward your dreams;
- Commit to where you are headed without holding yourself back.

Considering Your Transferable Skills

Some Asians may have experienced growing up in an environment where their parents expected them to follow a specific route for their career and expected the hard work to pay for itself throughout the years. Give yourself permission to reflect on your journey and consider your transferable skills if you do want to change your career path. Rather than waiting for something to happen, you are capable of taking action on your own. We will equip you with strategies and examples of how you can make this happen in your own life.

Personally, I never really knew what I wanted to be growing up, and I had no idea how to figure it out. My sister was the complete opposite. She knew she wanted to become a nurse since high school, and she is now a nurse practitioner. Through career quizzes, career counselors, and mentorships, I still was undecided about my career until college forced me to pick one. I selected marketing during my junior year in college since it piqued my interest due to the creativity and curiosity of the minds in that industry. After college, I pursued a career in marketing and advertising, and I never would have imagined changing my career to something else.

Eventually, however, I wanted to find a career that was more aligned with my values and interests. Following my curiosity, heart, and passion led me to discover what would be a more fulfilling career, and so I pivoted my career to learning and development. I found a job opening for a director role that I did not have the years of experience the employer required, but I went ahead and applied anyway, expressing my passion and transferable skills in the cover letter. Fortunately, they were interested in having a conversation with me to learn more about my experience. After four rounds of interviews, the employer made me an offer as a manager, creating a new role for me to join their organization. This was the first time in my career that an employer saw the value I brought to the table as well as my potential. My success landing the job was based on my pitch of my transferable skills.

Transferable skills are skills that you acquired and mastered in one job or industry that you can use in a new job or industry. You can acquire these skills during your education, internship, and work experience, and they may be transformed as tools to adapt in a new workplace. The following are examples of transferable skills, according to CareerCliff.com:

- Business strategy;
- Teamwork and leadership;
- Critical thinking;
- Adaptability and problem-solving;
- Data analysis;
- Creativity;
- Attention to detail.

Some examples of how to use your transferable skills to switch industries or jobs include the following:

- **Look at internal job postings:** Employers are looking to retain you as an employee, and if you see a job that is in a different department you may be interested in applying for, contact your human resources department and hiring manager to ask them about the opportunity and what skills of yours may be transferable.
- **Leverage your different background:** Know that your experience brings value to an employer as your different perspective could help the organization get to the next

level. For example, if you have worked in a large company, you could bring those best practices into a smaller company.

- **Consider relocating:** If you are open to relocating, you could consider looking for opportunities in a different location where they may not have your kind of talent in that area. Utilize tools like NerdWallet's cost of living calculator to compare your cost of living in different cities: https://www.nerdwallet.com/cost-of-living-calculator.

- **Improve your leadership role:** If you are looking to apply for leadership roles and do not have that experience in your current role, you could apply for positions on boards in professional organizations or your local community. Volunteer board work can add value to your leadership experience.

- **Invest in professional development:** Invest in yourself. Take online learning classes and workshops to take yourself to the next level that supports your career goals. Taking the initiative to learn new skills helps you stand out and will show hiring managers that you are being proactive to learn what you need for success in a new role.

The next section will cover how to navigate career pivots and how you would utilize your transferable skills to support your next stage in your career path.

Navigating Career Pivots

Career pivots happen more often than people talk about. According to the Bureau of Labor Statistics, Americans today average about 4½ years in a job. For younger generations, the job duration is about 2½ years.[1] This means people are switching jobs frequently. It is therefore critical to know how to create your own career path and tell your story as you most certainly will be transitioning from one role to the next every couple of years or so.

There is no magic button or rule for living life in a specific way, but it is critical to be responsible for your own career path, rather than having someone else tell you what to do or where they see you. If you want to pivot your career, you need to take action yourself and not wait for opportunities to arise or fall from the sky.

Many Asian Americans believe that all they need to do to be noticed is to work hard. This is not true. The reality check is that nobody will notice you until you wave your hand and demand to be noticed. You will not be able to successfully navigate a career pivot without being noticed. In the last chapter, you learned about how to craft your personal brand and own your story, and this is where you can apply those skills to elevate yourself to the next level in the workplace.

The National Association of Asian American Professionals (NAAAP) DC's webinar on "Pivoting Your Career and Switching Fields" reminds us that we need to take things into our own hands and know that we may fail a few times before getting it right. They even share inspirational Asian leaders who have noteworthy career pivots including Victoria Lai, a former government lawyer turned founder of Ice Cream Jubilee; Ken Jeong, a doctor who pursued acting and comedy; Dwayne Johnson, also known as "The Rock," a former football player and wrestler turned actor.[2] Although these are well-known examples, career pivots are more common than you may have imagined.

Reflecting on Your Career Path

You may find it difficult to know if it is the right time to change your career. And you may still want to keep growing on your current career trajectory. You are in control of what direction you want your path to go on. It is critical to know what your North Star is—that is, knowing your purpose in life that aligns with your values for what you want to do. In *Don't Stay in Your Lane*, Cynthia Pong shares a great temperature check for you to self-reflect on what is happening in your life. She suggests that you ask yourself the following questions:[3]

1. What are my top priorities for this stage of my life?
2. What's going well in my current work situation?
3. What's not going well?
4. What do my gut and intuition tell me about whether I should change careers?

Reflecting on your career path is a game changer that helps you see yourself from within. Think about not only your career but also key moments in your life that brought you to where you are and consider what the future you want to live in looks like. After you take the time to reflect, you will understand where to prioritize your time and energy.

Creating Your Own Opportunities

Trust the universe about where your unique career path is headed and remember that it is often not in the destination but in the journey itself that you are constantly creating your own opportunities. For example, on my journey, I became the president of my college chapter of the American Advertising Federation to hone in on my leadership skills. After college and early in my career, I joined the Young Professional Board for the Advertising Club of New York. When I pivoted to learning and development, I joined the Association for Talent Development NYC leadership board to build a network of talent development professionals. Because Asian Americans are rarely given the opportunity to work on assignments that develop their strategic and leadership skills, they must create their own opportunities as I did. This is a key example of how to disrupt corporate America for the benefit of all.

Interview with Ariba Jahan

Ariba Jahan is a product experience leader who is passionate about guiding the future of responsible technology. From earning a Bachelor of Science in biomechanical engineering at Syracuse University, to pursuing medical school, and ultimately embracing high-impact leadership in the start-up world, her journey perfectly highlights her conviction: the world of tomorrow is directly linked to the diversity and dedication of the minds shaping the technology of today. Ariba's career has been a testament to her versatility: She is the VP of Experience Strategy and Innovation at the Ad Council where she pioneered the nonprofit's current design innovation practice. She is an active keynote speaker for global tech conferences as well as for organizations like Vox Media, Etsy, and Hubspot. She is currently an adjunct professor at Parsons School of Design and has guest-lectured at places like Columbia University. In her free time, Ariba mentors young women in tech as part of her mission to bring more diverse, intersectional, and marginalized voices to positions of power and leadership. As an immigrant Bangladeshi woman with hearing loss, Ariba believes that the only path to a future that is mutually beneficial for all is to ensure our society, technology, and community are shaped by our lived experiences.

When did you know you wanted to change your career path?

I don't think I ever knew I wanted a career change. I just knew that every time my career path changed it was after a deep sense of unhappiness with whatever direction I was going in. In 2012, I was in medical school, and nothing felt aligned. I wasn't doing well, I was pretty unhappy, and I had no clarity about where I was going in my life. This was after I had already taken a year off to help my mom heal and recover from her cancer treatment. Growing up as an immigrant in America meant I was constantly reminded to perform academic excellence and attain career security. There was no room for "what if's?" or exploring other paths. But eventually, I stopped trying to make things that didn't serve me work, and I gave myself permission to leave a career I had invested in for a decade. Instead, I leaned into the power of reinvention.

How did you explain your transferable skills to your new employer?

This is something that changed over time. In the beginning, I only acknowledged specific skills like problem-solving, communication skills, and software competencies. I shied away from sharing my career pivot experience because I felt self-conscious about my path and how different it was from my colleagues or people often on conference stages.

But eventually, I began to see my skills in new contexts and discover more of my own transferable skills. For the last few years, I've actually started embracing the fact that I pivoted my career and began celebrating my path instead. I'm someone who can start from scratch; I'm resourceful; I can start and finish very complex projects; I can embrace ambiguity and can create experiments to explore possibilities.

I work well with people across different fields, and I'm familiar with the discomfort in change. The messiness of experimentation and exploration is where I shine. These are all really important skills that I developed working in different contexts and roles, but they only became visible to me when I embraced the journey I had taken.

What was your action plan to land a new job?

At the time, I didn't have one. I didn't even have a job in mind. In fact, I had no clue what could be next for me. Whenever I reach this place in life, a combination of two things happens: I go into survival mode, and I go into emergence mode.

Survival mode for me meant living in my mom's basement and focusing on how I could meet my basic human needs. Emergence mode allowed me to pursue my curiosity while exploring possibilities grounded in a sense of fulfillment and growth.

Being in survival mode is hard, and I want to recognize that "exploring careers" requires a level of financial privilege that looks different for everyone—whether you have savings that can help you float for a certain period of time or you have support from your family or community.

Here are some tactics I did, broken down by phases:

Initial Discovery

- Reconnected with classmates, friends and professors for advice and insights;
- Searched through Reddit, Facebook, and blogs to see what others did after med school or after a gap in a bio-mechanical engineering career;
- Went through job search sites and LinkedIn to get familiar with different job titles and descriptions;
- Stayed open to opportunities that were completely different from my past experiences.

Incremental Experimentation

- I took a job at a start-up so I could learn more about the New York start-up ecosystem and give myself a completely different experience away from medicine.
- Within my job at the start-up, I experimented with my role. By the time I left the organization, I had done operations, growth and scaling, onboarding and leading staff, teaching and coaching entrepreneurs, user research, and product management. Dabbling in so many different roles, helped me see my skills in a very different context as well as learn brand new skills.

Emergence

- In parallel I took courses I was interested in—Data Science, Product Management, as well as courses that had more probable job paths like QA Testing w/ C++.
- As I was getting exposed to the start-up space, I spoke with people working in all types of different roles to understand what they were doing and how it showed up in their contexts (industry, role, company).

As I learned more from being exposed to different conversations, courses, and insights, I looked for what sparked my curiosity and followed the ones I wanted to. Even now, I cultivate emergence and experimentation in my life, while unlearning survival mode.

What is your advice to someone interested in changing jobs to something new?

1. Figure out:
   - Is this a job change because you feel unsafe and need a really quick exit?
   - Is this a career exploration that you want to invite into your life?
   - How much financial resources do you need and have in order to do this shift? For how long?
2. Give yourself the permission to:
   - Let feelings of panic and being overwhelmed from the uncertainties coexist with the exhilaration of learning something new;
   - Follow sparks of curiosity but also abandon any sparks that no longer serve you;
   - Dive into courses, conversations, career research, and experimenting with jobs even if you don't feel like you know enough.
3. Don't wait for your imposter syndrome to go away. I personally don't think it actually goes away; it looks different at every stage of our lives. For me, I focused more on not letting the imposter syndrome hold too much power over my decisions.
4. Redefine career and success for yourself, and revisit that definition throughout your life. The factors of a career and a sense of success could look different for you at different phases, and that's wonderful.

How has being Asian affected your career?

For me, it's the intersectionality of being an immigrant in America, Bangladeshi, having a hearing disability, and growing up poor that impacted my educational journey, career path, and how I show up. I spent a great part of my school years feeling the pressure to assimilate without understanding how to. Instead, I made myself small, never embraced my culture beyond our household, endured microaggressions and racism, and rarely advocated for my accessibility needs. It's only within the last few years that I started feeling more ownership of my own lived experience, my journey, and my accessibility needs and felt the responsibility to share my own story.

Key Takeaways

- A trailblazer is a lifelong learner and pioneer who creates their own path for themselves and others to follow as they navigate a new path.
- Transferable skills are what makes you useful. They can be transformed as tools to adapt in a new workplace. They include critical thinking, adaptability, problem-solving, creativity, data analysis, teamwork, leadership, and more.

Reflections

- **Think about the life you want to live and take action to create it into your reality.**
  - o Imagine what your next chapter in your career journey will look like and what you need to do now to create that life.
  - o Listen to our interviewee, Ariba Jahan, in an Asians in Advertising podcast episode, Navigating Career Pivots

and Disability with the VP of Design at the Ad Council: https://apple.co/3HaJM1a.

- **Write down your transferable skills to have as your own personal toolkit.**
  o Review the examples of transferable skills and highlight the ones you possess. They might include communication, dependability, teamwork, organization, adaptability, leadership, empathy, decision-making, initiative, and technology https://www.indeed .com/career-advice/resumes-cover-letters/transferable-skills.
- **Know your North Star.**
  o Understand what your purpose in life is.
  o Align your career path with your values and what you want to do.

5

Finding Your Optimal Work-Life Balance

Bernice Chao

If you feel "burnout" setting in, if you feel demoralized and exhausted, it is best, for the sake of everyone, to withdraw and restore yourself.

—Dalai Lama, Buddhist teacher

HAVE YOU EVER described how you're feeling about work as "drowning"? If you have or currently are, chances are your work-life balance is out of alignment. In this chapter, we will talk about a few tools that will help you find the balance between your work life and personal life by talking through what matters and why. Work-life balance is the amount of time you spend on your career and working versus the time you spend with your loved ones and doing the things you enjoy. When creating a life of balance, you are creating a space in your life that will be open to new possibilities.

If you are knee-deep in work and frazzled due to looming deadlines, you may miss out on new, exciting opportunities because you may be in an unstable, unhealthy work environment. This chapter will discuss how to stay Zen in the midst of overwhelming responsibilities, and it will support and guide you in taking an actionable approach to your personal work-life balance. As a result, you will be able to show up more confidently, manage your priorities better, and create new opportunities to help yourself grow.

As Asians, we're generally taught to be hardworking to a fault. This may look like consistently putting in more work hours in our days, taking on more than we can manage, not saying no, or not giving ourselves time to unwind. If we aren't busy, then we feel as if we are not doing all we can to succeed, which can lead to burnout. Signs you could be burned out include exhaustion, dreading work, insomnia, depression, short temper, migraines, and illness. Constantly being plagued by these issues can create chronic stress, which can be a detriment not only to your physical health but to your mental health as well. (We will talk about this in the next chapter.)

Overwork is not a good thing, but it is prevalent in Asian culture. Workers in Asian countries work longer hours than in the Western world. In Asian countries such as Cambodia, Malaysia, Singapore, Bangladesh, Hong Kong, China, Vietnam, India, Philippines, and South Korea, employees reportedly work over 2,000 hours per year, compared to 1,700 hours per year in the United States.[1] A landmark study by the World Health Organization (WHO) and the International Labor Organization found that 745,000 people died in 2016 from stroke and ischemic heart disease as a direct result of having worked at least 55 hours a week.[2] This is why it is critical for you to understand the negative impact of overworking yourself. We are here to help you find the optimal work-life balance that will be healthy for your life.

Understanding the Negative Impact of Work-Life Imbalance

The impact of having your work and life unbalanced is more than just being unavailable or tired. Earlier in my career, I was at a job that had me overworked and they expected me to work on holidays. On New Year's Eve, I finished snowboarding with friends, and when I arrived at an area with cell reception, I received 12 voicemails from someone about a file that needed fixing. The matter was not urgent, and the person leaving the messages easily could have opened up the file and fixed it themselves. At the same job, I asked to take a week off after not taking a single day off for six months. The employer told me that it was not going to be possible because it was a busy season for the client. Being Asian and culturally taught to be nonconfrontational, it was hard for me to say no and voice my perspective to set boundaries with my work-life balance. I wanted to save face and avoid the shame of not being able to handle it all. In the end, I was pushed past my limits and knew I had to quit after only six months of working. Knowing what I know now, I would have left months sooner. It is not worth it to put all your energy into work and then when you walk into your personal life, you have nothing left to give from exhaustion.

There are many red flags that should alert you to the fact that your life is unbalanced. These include working too many hours, sacrificing your health and well-being, taking time away from personal relationships, and thinking about work all the time.

Working Too Many Hours

When you are exhausted, you are not at your best, and your work and productivity will go down. You are probably putting in too many hours if you are working in excess of 40 hours per week, depending on your profession. Overwork leads to burnout, which is dangerous. If you are always getting in early and working late, you may be working too many hours. We have heard stories about employees who will pull all-nighters for work and not get any sleep or sleep over in the office due to work deadlines. This behavior would not be acceptable in a healthy work environment. We encourage you to communicate boundaries with your employer to avoid this from happening. It is important to be fully recharged at the start of each workday.

Sacrificing Your Health and Well-Being

No job is worth the deterioration of your health and well-being. A Stanford-educated litigator learned this the hard way. At a mid-sized law firm, she worked 17-hour days and all-nighters and was constantly on call. For several years, she had accepted her job's effect on her mental and physical health. Despite changes to her diet and exercise, as well as adding meditation to her daily routine, her blood sugar and cholesterol numbers kept going up, and her sleep problems worsened. The idea that her ambition and lack of boundaries were causing *irreversible* damage was a shock to her. In three weeks, three doctors and a therapist told her she needed to drastically reduce her stress levels, with one doctor commenting that if she didn't, she'd suffer "permanent negative effects." She switched to working two to three days a week, with a strict "no email outside of working hours" policy. She finally learned to prioritize her health and well-being.

According to *Medical News Today*, individuals who work 55 hours or more per week have a 1.3 times higher risk of stroke than those working standard hours.[3] Stress contributes to many physical and mental health problems, such as high blood pressure, heart disease, gastrointestinal problems, diabetes, asthma, depression, anxiety, and insomnia. When you start to realize that the cause of these problems may be from work, you will recognize the urgency of negotiating your workload and hours to a reasonable level in order to improve your health and well-being.

Taking Time Away from Personal Relationships

I worked for an employer where I was overworked and had to decline a friend's wedding in India, tons of dinners with friends, and time with my family. Being too busy can cause you to skip social events or take away quality time with your friends and family. Personal relationships need to be nurtured; by taking away quality interactions, you will grow distant or miss major milestones. If you are starting to notice that you are canceling plans and have less of a social life, it may be a sign that you are putting your job first, resulting in a work-life imbalance.

Thinking About Work All the Time

There is a difference between loving the work you do and thinking about work all the time. Your brain needs to take a rest to recharge from work. You do not want to be the person who is always talking about work or constantly checking work emails after work hours. If you are thinking about work around the clock or lose attention from a conversation because you're worried about a work project, you may need to consider the changes you need to improve your work-life balance. When you're with your family and friends, you should be present in the moment with them rather than focusing on work.

Prioritizing a Healthy Self-Care Lifestyle

Now that you understand some of the negative impacts of a work-life imbalance, it is critical to prioritize a healthy self-care lifestyle. Making sure that your body's basic needs are being met emotionally, physically, and spiritually will ensure that you function at your peak. You will not be able to take on tasks at work if the foundations of your body are weak. What you put into your body is like the gas you put into your car to accelerate and run smoothly. Essentially, your health is nonnegotiable. You must focus on it and consider being more intentional when it comes to ramping up your self-care.

In a survey by the Bureau of Labor Statistics, 83 percent of respondents said they spent no time during the day relaxing or thinking.[4] You do not want to be part of that 83 percent. What follows are some suggestions for changing and improving your emotional, physical, and spiritual self-care habits. They will support you in taking better care of your health.

- **Emotional self-care activities:**
  o Therapy;
  o Listening to music;
  o Writing a gratitude journal;
  o Positive self-talk.
- **Physical self-care activities:**
  o Exercise;

o Getting enough sleep;
o Eating well.
- **Spiritual self-care activities:**
o Meditation;
o Observing nature;
o Practicing acts of kindness.

These are only a few suggestions of how you can start leveling up your self-care. We recommend that you create your own list for what works for you. Try different activities and see what resonates. You can also ask a friend if they want to be your self-care accountability partner. You can create a healthy routine and check in with each other to see how you both are taking care of yourselves.

Learning to Say No

As you begin to prioritize a healthy lifestyle, you will also start to set more boundaries for yourself. One of the keys you need to unlock when building a better work-life balance is learning that it is okay to say no. A few years ago, I was asked if I wanted to be a founding member of a start-up meditation app called Evenflow that used psychological insights for a long-term benefit. Even though I was overwhelmed at work, the app founder was a friend and I did not feel like I could say no to the overwhelming multitude of pressing app needs. For some reason, I thought if I worked hard enough, I would be able to handle the extra work and not disappoint the people around me. However, I was drowning from working before and after normal work hours along with working on weekends. My relationship with my family, and friends suffered due to how anxious I was.

It finally dawned on me that I wasn't capable of doing more and that I finally had to say no and jump ship. Saying no more often can free yourself from obligations that don't benefit you.

What you choose to not take on is as important as what you decide to do. Managing your time and energy is crucial to living a more fulfilling life. The quicker you realize what's important and what needs to be prioritized, the quicker it will be to cut out things that are extraneous and do not matter. It takes practice to say no, and here are some ways to help you get started:

- **Enjoy what you do:** Ensure that you love and enjoy every aspect of the things you take on. Another way to judge if you should do a task is to ask yourself, "Do I *actually* want to do it?" or "Does it make me happy doing it?" You need to enjoy the tasks that you are doing to have the energy to want to do them.
- **Manage expectations:** Be clear when communicating deadlines and deliverables for your workload. Let your team and key stakeholders know if a deadline cannot be met with the reason or alternative solution.
- **Delegate the work:** See if there are ways to make your work situation easier by delegating work to someone else if possible. The work you want to delegate may not be suited for you but may be a great opportunity for someone else. Delegation is a way for both you and your team to grow.

Taking Action on Your Work-Life Balance

There is no one way to have the ideal work-life balance because each of us has different priorities that can change throughout our life. Finding the ideal work-life balance is not a one-time endeavor; it's something that needs to be constantly evaluated and rebalanced. Instead of thinking about it as work-life *balance*, you can think about it as work-life *blend*—it is how you begin to prioritize what is really important to you and decide how to integrate it into your life. You can take action to assess where you are today and reflect on where you want to be to manifest your own ideal work-life balance.

Managing Your Workload

Begin the journey of finding your optimal work-life balance by prioritizing what needs to be done first to manage your current workload. Start by creating a "brain dump" list of everything you are working on. Then label each task as high priority, mid priority, or low priority with deadlines for each one. This will give you a visual of your priorities, keeping you focused rather than being overwhelmed and not knowing where to begin. It is best to break down projects into baby steps and milestones to make them more manageable.

Evaluating Where You Want to Be

Next, think about what else adds holistic value to your life. We have created a chart to help you. In it, we have priority pillars that include career, family, self-growth, physical body, relaxation, and relationships. You can tailor these pillars specifically for yourself and your individual needs. The chart provides a great way to visually represent where you want to spend the bulk of your energy.

Categories

1. **Career:** Advancing your career or business objectives;
2. **Family:** Strengthening ties with your family;

3. **Self-growth:** Developing your mind, reading books, and taking classes;
4. **Physical body:** Improving your health and well-being;
5. **Relaxation:** Mental time off, meditation, and mindfulness;
6. **Relationships:** Nurturing relationships with friends and co-workers;
7. **Other:** Fill in your own.

	Rank Where You Are 1 = lowest / 5 = highest	Rank Where You Want to Be 1 = lowest / 5 = highest
Career		
Family		
Self-Growth		
Physical Body		
Relaxation		
Relationships		
Other _____		

Using this chart, rank where you are and where you want to be, with 1 being the lowest and 5 being the highest. Ask yourself: How does looking at this make me feel? What things are in my way to move from one column to another? Have I been prioritizing things that don't fit in my overall plan? You can utilize this chart at different stages of your life or access it frequently to help you assess if you are on track for what you want to focus your time and energy on when creating an optimal work-life balance.

Leading by Example

As a leader in the workplace who continues to focus on improving yourself, you can set an example for colleagues around you by prioritizing your own healthy work-life balance. Your behavior will inspire others and help cultivate a great and enjoyable workplace for everyone.

To help you get started, here are some examples of how to lead this journey by example:

- **Taking time off:** When you take time off, you show your employees that it is okay to take time for themselves. Encourage people to use their paid time off to take breaks and recharge, whether it is for a mental health day, staycation, traveling, spending time with family, or personal time to do anything they want away from work. Make sure you are not checking work emails when out of the office to set the example for your team of what time off really looks like.
- **Setting boundaries:** Communicate to your team what work expectations are from start to end time. If you catch your team working late hours, check in to see why.
- **Creating lunch blocks or breaks:** Break the work culture of back-to-back meetings by making sure you have lunches blocked along with necessary breaks in your day to recharge. You can also set a "No Friday afternoon meeting" rule.
- **Communicating workloads:** As a manager, you should make sure there is open communication with the team about managing workloads across the team; communication should be clear about deadlines and deliverables. Try to cross-train your team with tasks to ensure that

when people take time off, their work can be completed by other team members.

Interview with Bonnie Wan

Bonnie Wan is a partner and head of brand strategy at Goodby Silverstein & Partners and is the author of *The Life Brief: Creative Strategies for No Regrets Living*. Featured in Fast Company, Well + Good, Goop, and Jane Goodall's Activating Hope Summit, she helps people live with greater clarity, creativity, and courage. Bonnie is a graduate of NYU. She lives in San Anselmo, California, with her husband, four kids, and Charlie, the dog.

What has helped you the most to find work and life balance?

The word *balance* is a tricky one for me. I'm not sure I ever achieve true balance. But I do strive to braid together the parts of my life that matter most to me, while simultaneously cutting out the distractions and drama that get in the way. As a wife, mother of four, agency leader, client strategist, and author, I practice a few critical principles that keep me sane and centered. I call these *practices* because I do them with regularity, and they get easier the more I do them.

- **Hyper-presence.** If there is one game-changing practice in my life (besides *The Life Brief*), this is it. It's absolute focus and attention on what I'm doing and who I'm with right NOW. It's a sort of active meditation in the moment. I find that when I am present and available, I not only accomplish amazing things in slivers of time, but I also eliminate the stress and worry that comes from replaying the past or fretting about the future.

- **Radical distillation and prioritization.** As a career strategist, I have over three decades of practice in the art of surgical distillation—cutting through the B.S. and getting to the heart of what matters most. This is the essence of *The Life Brief* practice I've created. I now teach everyday people how to get sharp and clear about the life they want, so that they can radically prioritize and act on what matters most to them.
- **Push. Pause. Play.** I try to be as serious about my pauses and play as I am about pushes and productivity. I try to reward myself, even in the smallest of ways, for the big pushes I'm responsible for delivering with my family as the primary breadwinner, cook, and cuddler; as an agency leader and department head; and as an author, speaker, and coach. I recently took five days to myself, renting a tiny cabin in the woods, to write and nourish myself. It was hard to do and I was racked with guilt leading up to it. Yet the reward was immeasurable. I also do this in the tiny of ways every day. It could be lingering in bed without my phone for 5 or 15 minutes longer. It could be playing hooky for 30 minutes to take a mid-afternoon bath before the kids get home from school. It could be a Sunday stroll in the farmer's market.

Lastly, I'm a recovering perfectionist. While I still aim for high outcomes, I have learned to let go of setting impossible standards for myself and those around me. Letting go of perfectionism has created more time and spaciousness for relationships, creativity, and restoration.

How do you prioritize self-care?

Juggling leadership, four kids, and authoring a book means that self-care comes in small but frequent slivers of "sandwich time"—in between pushes. I reward every big push with either a pause or play. Pauses can include just a few minutes of quiet or a long soak. Play can be a movie or a stroll around the neighborhood with my youngest daughter and dog. Regardless of how I spend it, the key is keeping it small and simple . . . otherwise it won't happen.

How can you lead an example of work-life balance as a leader?

Work has invaded every corner of our lives. I joke that my teams spend more time in my bedroom with me than my husband! In response, I've become strict about blocking off time in my daily schedule for lunch, EOD workouts, and Do Not Disturb hours. I don't send (or check) after-hour and weekend emails or texts. The hardest habit to break in 2020 and 2021 was working through vacations as our business was so volatile during the pandemic. This year that has changed. My time-off is now sacred and I'm about to take four weeks off to celebrate my son's high school graduation.

How has being Asian affected your career?

I immigrated to the US from Taiwan at six years old. My parents were part of a generation who believed that the more "Americanized" their children were, the more opportunity and success we would have available to us. This blending in began with my new name. My parents came out of the movie Bonnie & Clyde with Faye Dunaway and Warren Beatty, and named me Bonnie and my little brother Clyde. Thankfully, on the good advice of family friends, they changed Clyde to Ken which phonetically fit better with my brother's Chinese name. The casual yet cutting racism I endured in my early school years further pushed me toward a path of assimilation, making way for career breakthroughs while enduring personal costs.

Since 2020, I have worked to reconcile and re-integrate my Chinese roots and heritage. It has been a hard but rewarding road—shaping my actions as a parent, leader, teacher, and friend. My fellow strategy partner and dear friend, Christine Chen, said, "We cannot see others until we see ourselves." This wisdom stirs within me as I reclaim my identity and pride in being AAPI.

Key Takeaways

- Prioritize a healthy lifestyle to make sure your body's basic needs are met emotionally, physically, and spiritually.
- Consider the red flags for work-life imbalance including working too many hours, decreasing your well-being, neglecting your personal social life, and thinking about work all the time.
- Create a tasks list and sort it by high priority, mid priority, and low priority. It will help you focus on what's most important.
- Evaluate where you are and where you want to be with priority pillars.

Reflections

- Create your own toolkit of a healthy self-care lifestyle with emotional, physical, and spiritual activities. Here are a few examples:
  1. **Emotional:** Book your next therapist appointment to process your feelings and prioritize your mental health.
  2. **Physical:** Start a new workout routine to challenge your body.
  3. **Spiritual:** Try meditation apps like Headspace, Calm, and The Shine.
- Think about how you are leading by example to showcase a positive work-life balance.
  - Take time off for your mental health.
  - Communicate boundaries for work hours and non-negotiables based on your priority pillars.
  - Intentionally create blocks in your work calendar for breaks in the day to recharge.
- When was the last time you delegated your workload to someone else at work?
  - Utilize a step-by-step guide to help you learn how to delegate tasks at: https://online.hbs.edu/blog/post/how-to-delegate-effectively

6

Prioritizing Your Mental Health

Jessalin Lam

*Be present with the moment. Be present with your needs. Show
yourself kindness and grace. Tune out the external world and tune
in on how you're doing and feeling. You have to create space and
cultivate kindness toward yourself in order to do the same
for others.*
—Sara Porritt, chief diversity and inclusion officer, Omnicom
Media Group

LET'S BEGIN BY defining what mental health means and why
it is important to prioritize. According to the World Health
Organization, *mental health* includes our emotional, psychological, and social well-being. It affects how we think, feel,
and act. It also helps determine how we handle stress, relate
to others, and make healthy choices.[1]

Talking about the importance and benefits of mental
health is critical for all people, but especially so for the Asian
community. Culturally, Asian Americans frown on the idea
of mental health or even making time for yourself. We are

93

taught to take care of our elders, siblings, and everyone around us. This chapter will share the powerful and positive impacts of how prioritizing your mental health will change your life, enabling you to become more mindful in your everyday life, personally and professionally. Leveling up your mental health will not only help you become more visible, it will also allow you to live your life in a holistic and healthier way.

Understanding the Reality of Mental Health for Asians

It is crucial to acknowledge the importance for Asian Americans to break the stigma surrounding mental health and start to actively talk about it while also providing resources and solutions for Asian Americans. Your mental health state has a significant impact on all areas of your life. We need to change the narrative to let people know it is okay to not be okay, to address mental health concerns, and to ask for professional help when needed.

When it comes to Asian Americans, the American Psychological Association shared the following statistics on suicide-related outcomes due to mental illness, social factors, and more:

- Among all Asian Americans, those aged 20–24 had the highest suicide rate.
- Suicide was the 8th leading cause of death for Asian Americans, whereas it was the 11th leading cause of death for all racial groups combined.
- Asian American college students had a higher rate of suicidal thoughts than white college students.

- US-born Asian American women had a higher lifetime rate of suicidal thoughts (15.9 percent) than that of the general US population (13.5 percent).[2]

Despair among Asian Americans is clearly a problem. But what can we do? We can start by breaking down some of the stereotypes common among the Asian American community.

Asking for Help Is a Sign of Weakness

When we break it down to better understand why Asian Americans may not go to therapy, it is due to the underlying fear that getting mental health treatment means you are "weak" or, worse, "crazy." If you admit you need help, a strong sense of fear or shame might be experienced.[3]

According to the Substance Abuse and Mental Health Services Administration (SAMHSA), Asian Americans are less likely to reach out for help than other races and ethnic groups due to religious and cultural values as well as language barriers.[4] Only 8.6 percent of Asian Americans typically seek any type of mental health services compared to nearly 18 percent of the general population nationwide.[5]

Solution: Reframe the way you think about asking for help as a sign of strength, confidence, and resourcefulness. You have the power to change your life, evolve, and heal yourself from the benefit of therapy. In reality, the true weakness is not asking for help as the person who will suffer the most is you.

Burdening People with Your Emotions Is Unnecessary

Many Asians believe it is a burden to share emotions or problems with a stranger, especially someone you pay. Many

Asian Americans grow up in households where everyone hides their emotions. Pretending everything is okay and being silent are perceived as strengths, which they are not.

Solution: It is not safe or healthy to keep all your emotions bottled up inside yourself. A great therapist will be able to ask you the right questions to help you discover things you may not have thought about most of your life and guide you in a better light for how to move forward. As Warren Buffet says, "By far the best investment you can make is in yourself."

Talking to Therapists Does Not Help Us

Finding a good therapist can be extremely difficult, and if you had a bad experience with one, you may end up generalizing that therapy is not helpful. Some therapists may not understand your specific situation, culture, and heritage. This does not mean you need to stop looking for help.

Solution: You will want to consider looking for a mental health professional who truly understands your Asian cultural background and specific situation. There are plenty of resources out there to help you find an Asian therapist including the Asian Mental Health Collective, the Yellow Chair Collective, Inclusive Therapists, Psychology Today, and South Asian Therapists.

Breaking the Stigma of Mental Health in the Workplace

Now that you know that Asians are not taught to lean on mental health resources to support them in life, let's dive into an example of my own. I was never taught about mental health growing up, and it was always unsaid that you should pretend everything was great even if there was a problem. My family cared about what other people thought and saving face—avoiding having other people lose respect for you—was paramount. Unfortunately, these attitudes did affect me up until I became an adult and had to unlearn them. My first time going to therapy took place in 2018. That was the year I focused on my mental health and self-care. It was all new and unknown to me, but I was open to trying it to help me improve how I was handling life. In one of my first therapy sessions, after I shared a personal story that triggered me to cry, the therapist asked how I was feeling, and my autopilot response was "I'm okay," while I was still wiping away my tears. She responded with, "It's okay to not be okay. Your feelings are valid." It was surprisingly my first time that someone had said this to me.

> I want to pass this message along to you: It is actually healthy to admit you are not okay, give yourself permission to feel all the emotions you are going through, and when you are ready, take the time to reflect on what you would like to do about it.

My earlier example was related to a personal situation I was dealing with for my own healing journey, but I have also spoken to my therapist about work problems. According to The American Institute of Stress, 83 percent of US workers suffer from work-related stress.[6] I have experienced being stressed and burdened from toxic workplaces where I would miss my stop going home, dread waking up to go to work on a daily basis, or find myself not knowing what to do next. My therapist guided me in unpacking my situation and thinking more about what I had control over.

Working on your mental health makes you stronger and strengthens the way your mind tackles and overcomes challenges. It even builds your resilience to bounce back and stay grounded when you are in a better headspace. It has worked for me.

Here are some ways to break the stigma of mental health in the workplace:

- Take mental health days;
- Talk about the benefits of your therapist;
- Educate others by sharing mental health resources;
- Show compassion when someone shares their mental health experiences.

Workplace stress contributes to a critical part of the general mental health crisis. If we all work toward breaking the stigma surrounding mental health, our workplaces will become healthier environments to work in. Healthy workplaces lead to increased employee engagement, retention, and productivity along with a deeper sense of community and belonging.

Interview with Cassandra Lam

Cassandra Lam is a Vietnamese American trauma-informed facilitator, somatic healing practitioner, and community builder. As a neurodivergent and empathic daughter of refugees, Cassandra's passion lies in creating spaces of safety, care, and healing for historically marginalized peoples. Her teachings are informed by 10 years of personal practice in the healing arts, 300+ hours of training in mindfulness, politicized somatics, and trauma, and a commitment to healing justice principles. As chief executive officer and co-founder of The Cosmos, she creates community, content, and experiences for Asian women in America. She graduated from the University of California, Los Angeles, with a bachelor's degree in political science.

Could you share more about your journey with mental health and what led you to your career path?

I was born in Covina, California, as the oldest daughter of Vietnamese boat refugees. Raised by parents with undiagnosed mental illness and untreated PTSD [post-traumatic stress disorder], I grew up a sensitive child in an unsafe environment defined by domestic violence, child abuse, and narcissism. It was a very lonely childhood experience because not only has my dad been estranged from his siblings for most of my life, but he also pressured my mom to disconnect—or at least maintain a large distance—with her family too. This created an environment ruled by secrecy, shame, and isolation—ingredients that enable abuse to fester.

These painful experiences are what sparked my obsession with somatics—a holistic methodology for individual and collective liberation that views the body as an essential site for change, learning, and transformation—as a way to heal. Through somatics and mindfulness, I learned to reclaim my authentic self and body from the tyranny of trauma. As I dove deeper into research on Asian American mental health, my personal experience, and my training as a practitioner, I learned that many Asian folks, like me, related to themselves and/or their mental health from this body-based lens. It was also affirming to discover that this is because *somatics IS Asian culture!* (https://tadahozumi.com/on-cultural-somatics-being-an-asian-practice/) I wish to do my small part to help reclaim this body of work from white supremacy and to share this ancestral wisdom with our community.

My passion for facilitating spaces for Asian women and femmes to learn and practice somatic healing practices, in an accessible way and in community, comes from my own experiences of struggling to afford the mental health care I desperately needed. I've been uninsured or underinsured, underpaid, and under immense stress at many points in my life. Much of my career can be viewed as me trying to become what I needed to heal.

Meanwhile there aren't enough AAPI therapists to meet the demand as it is, and you can only work with a therapist if you have the financial privilege to afford it. So where do uninsured folks go? Where do low-income folks go? Where do undocumented folks go?

Beyond that, I also struggle with the hyper-individualized mental healthcare model. While I believe in the value of a 1:1 therapeutic relationship, I don't think it's a complete solution because we are social creatures living in an interdependent world. In my work at The Cosmos, I have heard from many Asian women and femmes who feel isolated and struggle after going through a significant change, such as breaking up with a toxic partner or healing intergenerational trauma, because they do not have access to the support systems they need to sustain that change in their everyday life. Without that support, we are likely to fall back to old and potentially harmful or unhealthy ways of being because it is deeply painful to not feel seen or supported as the new you.

What tips or best practices do you have when it comes to prioritizing positive mental health?

If I were to speak to my younger self, here is the advice I would share to help her care for her mental health:

- Read *Healing Night: The Science and Spirit of Sleeping, Dreaming, and Awakening* by Rubin Naiman, PhD, and *Why We Sleep* by Matthew Walker, PhD. These two books will dispel all the false notions around sleep that you inherited from society and help you actually realign to a lifestyle that honors your body's natural need for rest and sleep.

- Create a morning ritual that enables you to gift yourself the GIFT OF YOUR SELF: The first few hours upon waking are some of the most potent and special hours of the day. Since we're emerging from sleep, we tend to be our most refreshed, clear-eyed, self-reflective, and creative in these hours. So much of our anxiety, stress, insomnia, and general malaise can come from the ways in which we may unconsciously be giving ourselves away or allowing our attention and energy to be sapped dry.
- You cannot multitask as well as you think you can. If you don't believe me, read the science on it! Also, multitasking is contributing to your anxiety. There is beauty and value in doing one thing at a time, with presence, intention, and care.
- Log off the computer at a reasonable time—even if you didn't finish everything on your to-do list: You don't have to be a superhero, and unless you work in the emergency room, it probably is not as urgent as it may feel. In many cases, deadlines and meetings can be rescheduled. However, you only have one body! So, it's important to learn how to really listen for its cues.
- Build a loving support system for yourself. It doesn't have to be big! Even just a couple friends who you feel really seen and heard by, comfortable to be yourself around, and who invest in you as much as you invest in them can go a long, long way. As someone who could never rely on family for support or love, it's

always been friends and community that have held me. Thanks to the Internet, there are so many amazing communities where you can dip your toe in to find your people in a COVID-safe way!

What do you think needs to change to break the stigma surrounding mental health in the Asian community?

I might be biased since I spend a lot of time with Millennial and Gen-Z Asian folks in both my personal and professional life, but it feels like we've made significant strides in breaking the stigma on mental health these past few years! The younger generation is trailblazing and leading the way in terms of having more open, honest, and solutions-oriented conversations on mental health. Whether I'm hanging out with my friends, holding space for Cosmos community members, or facilitating healing sessions or workshops for BIPOC [Black, Indigenous, and People of Color] or AAPI ERGs [employee resource groups] in corporate workplaces, mental health seems to be top of mind, which is very heartening. So, I name this because I think it's worthy of celebration and many people and organizations played a role in this cultural shift.

However, that doesn't mean that everyone in the Asian community feels safe or supported in disclosing their mental health status, asking for help, or navigating the mental health care system. Low-income, undocumented, disabled, queer and trans, non-English speaking, and elderly Asians still face significant barriers to accessing culturally sensitive and affordable care.

I am also thinking of the many AAPI folks I know, both personally and in my line of work, who are proud to be seeking mental health care, but who still feel like they need to hide it from their family.

What are some of your own self-care routines you could share with our community?

I don't believe self-care is one-size-fits-all as we're each unique and navigating many things, both visible and invisible, so please take anything I share with a grain of salt. Ultimately, your body will be the most accurate detector of what resonates and works for you.

Here are some aspects of my day-to-day self-care routine:

- I have a two-hour morning ritual that I commit to completing before I respond to *anyone*—including text messages from family, news or content online, my email inboxes, work, or social media.
- I do some combination of meditation, movement (stretching, yoga, breathwork, or dancing in front of a mirror with my favorite songs blasting), and journaling every single day. It doesn't have to be long; it just has to happen!
- I no longer consume the news daily. Instead, I choose a specific time during the week when I want to engage with the news and trust that my community will share anything that I should know with me.
- I take a walk outside at least once a day. I am still trying to get into a better habit of doing this because the inertia of just staying in the apartment can be so strong!
- I take baths regularly—at least once a week. But if I'm having a bad day or feeling back pain, I'll draw upon this tool too. Being in a pool of warm water can be deeply nourishing for a weary body.

- I hold a lot of tension in my body that can lead to pain, so my partner and I bought a portable massage table for our apartment.

What resources would you recommend for people related to mental health?

If you're an Asian woman or femme, I would love to invite you to join The Cosmos community at an upcoming virtual or in-person event in NYC! Otherwise, I'd recommend finding a community where people who share your identity are actively discussing mental health, especially if you don't have folks in your life that you feel safe talking about it with. Some AAPI mental health communities I know of are The Cosmos (@jointhecosmos), Brown Girl Therapy (@browngirltherapy), Asian Mental Health Collective (@asianmentalhealthcollective), Asian Mental Health Project (@asianmentalhealthproject), and Asians Do Therapy (@asiansdotherapy).

The other resources I'd like to recommend are book recommendations that have really helped me, including:
- *The Body Keeps the Score* by Bessel van der Kolk;
- *My Grandmother's Hands: Racialized Trauma and the Pathway to Mending Our Hearts and Bodies* by Resmaa Menakem, MSW LICSW SEP;
- *What My Bones Know* by Stephanie Foo;
- *No Mud, No Lotus: The Art of Transforming Suffering* by Thich Nhat Hanh;
- *When Things Fall Apart: Heart Advice for Difficult Times* by Pema Chodron;

- *Healing Night: The Science and Spirit of Sleeping, Dreaming, and Awakening* by Dr. Rubin Naiman;
- *Why We Sleep* by Matthew Walker.

Key Takeaways

- Suicide was the eighth leading cause of death for Asian Americans. Asian Americans need to actively talk about mental health and be provided with solutions to support them.
- The common stereotypes that need breaking when it comes to mental health among the Asian American community include asking for help is a sign of weakness, burdening people with your emotions is unnecessary, and talking to therapists does not help.
- To break the stigma of mental health in the workplace, you can take mental health days, talk about benefits of your therapy, and share mental health resources.

Reflections

Please note that the suggestions here are not a substitute for professional help.

- **Evaluate the different types of therapy from which you can choose.**
  o Common types of therapy include psychodynamic, behavioral, CBT, and humanistic. Read more at: https://www.healthline.com/health/types-of-therapy.
- **Book an appointment with a therapist to check on your mental health and make use of the following resources:**
  o Asian Mental Health Collective
  o The Yellow Chair Collective

- o Inclusive Therapists
- o ZenCare
- o South Asian Therapists
- o South Asian Mental Health Initiative and Network
- **Educate yourself on the well-being of Asian American communities.**
  - o The Asian American Psychological Association (AAPA) focuses on using research, education, policy, and professional practice to advance the mental health of Asian Americans https://aapaonline.org/.
  - o The National Asian American Pacific Islander Mental Health Association (NAAPIMHA) is a resource provider for mental health services for Asian Americans, Pacific Islanders, and Native Hawaiians. The organization provides a resource list of state-level programs designed to meet AAPI-community mental health needs https://www.naapimha.org/aanhpi-service-providers.
  - o The National Alliance on Mental Illness (NAMI) provides AAPI resources with an overview on barriers including mental health stigma, language barriers, and lack of culturally competent providers along with seminars and support groups https://www.nami.org/Your-Journey/Identity-and-Cultural-Dimensions/Asian-American-and-Pacific-Islander.
  - o The National Queer Asian Pacific Islander Alliance (NQAPIA) brings together lesbian, gay, bisexual, and transgender (LGBT) Asian American, South Asian, Southeast Asian, and Pacific Islander (AAPI) organizations and provides education, leadership development, collaboration, and visibility to help challenge racism and anti-LGBTQ bias https://www.nqapia.org/.

- **Assess your mental health.**
  - o Take Mental Health America's free online screening: https://screening.mhanational.org/screening-tools/ or Psychology Today's Mental Health Assessment: https://www.psychologytoday.com/us/tests/health/ mental-health-assessment.

PART

II

Working with Others

7

Addressing Microaggressions

Bernice Chao

As a society, we can't hide from the future; we have to build and own it.

—Andrew Yang, American businessman and
political candidate

WHEN I WAS in college, I went to the local Humane Society to adopt a kitten. While I was signing the paperwork, I was asked by the director of the shelter, "What will happen to the animal when you return to your home country?" I was so taken aback because it was such a strange question when all I had ever known was America. This *is* my country, and I don't know life as a non-American. This shelter worker basically made the snap judgment, based on my visual appearance alone, that I was a foreigner. Presuming this shelter worker was simply looking out for what was best for the animal, she most likely didn't realize what she said was off-putting, but this is a real-life example of how microaggressions can have a strong impact on the victim of the microaggression. More than a quarter of Americans have experienced a microaggression at work and 36 percent have witnessed one.[1]

This chapter will teach you how to recognize when microaggressions occur, show you step-by-step ways to handle the situation, and give you resources that you can share with co-workers and corporations so that they can become supportive allies. You will leave this chapter with the proper tools to educate and shift perceptions in the workplace, ultimately making a better work environment for all to enjoy.

Defining Microaggression

Let's start with what a microaggression is. The *Merriam Webster Dictionary* defines *microaggression* as "as a comment or action that subtly and often unconsciously or unintentionally expresses a prejudiced attitude toward a member of a marginalized group, such as a racial minority." Psychologist Derald Wing Sue calls microaggressions the "everyday slights, indignities, insults, put downs and invalidations" that people from marginalized communities experience on a regular basis.[2] Often microaggressions are subtle; the person delivering the microaggression may not even know what they're saying is offensive when saying it. They might think what they are saying is funny.

Here are some common microaggressions that Asian Americans might face:

- No, but where are you really from?
- You speak English so well!
- Where were you born?

- You all look alike.
- You're so exotic looking.
- Your lunch smells weird.
- You must be good at math.
- Are you a good driver?
- My friend (or wife or husband or . . .) is Asian.
- When I look at you, I don't see color.

Some of these phrases may seem like the person is giving a compliment, such as "You speak English so well" or "You're so exotic looking"; however, the message behind these microaggressions is that the person is a foreigner. Other microaggressions such as "You must be good at math" or "Are you a good driver?" are creating blanket statements based on a person's race. The most subtle of the bunch is "When I look at you, I don't see color"; the speaker here is actually denying the person of color's ethnic experiences. No matter what the context of these examples, it shows how the receiver is treated differently purely on the basis of looking Asian.

Understanding the Reality of Microaggressions

To explain why microaggressions are so harmful, we need to start at the root of microaggressions. The "Yellow Peril" stereotype of the late nineteenth century depicted people of East and Southeast Asia as a danger to the western world. This term was coined to alienate a group of people based on their race alone; it was not tied to any source of danger, but instead reflected an existential fear of faceless, nameless hordes of yellow people.[3] The idea was that Asians were taking career opportunities from "true" Americans. To prevent this from happening, laws were enacted to take away rights, including the Chinese Exclusion Act of 1882, which banned Chinese laborers from entering the United States, and then eventually the National Origins Act of 1924 which banned people from all of Asia.

Identifying Asians as Foreigners

Though America has now allowed immigration from Asian nations, the idea that Asians can be accepted as fully American was never fully adopted, making Asians perpetually foreigners no matter how successful they are. Even when Asians are born in the United States, they are treated differently—as if they are not Americans. As John Cho wrote in a *Los Angeles Times* op-ed, "Our belonging is conditional."[4] A moment may come along to remind you that your race defines you above all else. It might be a small moment, like a salesperson greeting you in a different dialect as they make assumptions on where you're from. "Microaggressions are really meant to make people feel like lesser human beings," says Dr. Warren Ng, child and adolescent psychiatrist at Columbia University. "There's another term for microaggressions: Death by a thousand cuts. I think that description really does speak to the cumulative effects."[5]

Affecting the Safety of the Asian Community

Although the term *micro* in *microaggressions* may mean "small," when compounded, they can become *macro*, with major effects on the lives they afflict. The negative impact on the Asian community continues to increase. According to Stop AAPI Hate, from March 19, 2020, to September 30, 2021, there were a total of 10,370 hate incidents against

Asian American and Pacific Islander people. A majority of these incidents took place in spaces open to the public, and 62 percent of these hate incidents were reported by women.[6] Asian Americans have not found it safe to commute to the workplace due to these hate incidents—these microaggressions are harmful, and we need to take a more proactive approach to address them.

Increasing Stress Levels

Studies have shown that microaggressions can increase stress levels, negatively affect self-esteem and psychological well-being, and create and perpetuate systemic inequities in education, the workplace, and health care.[7] It clearly does not benefit your health to experience microaggressions in the workplace. Stop AAPI Hate reported that during this pandemic, 1 in 3 Asian and Asian American young adults reported clinically elevated symptoms of depression and general anxiety, and 1 in 4 reported a PTSD diagnosis.[8] At a minimum, with increased stress levels, productivity and happiness at work decline, resulting in a negative impact on mental health. The Substance Abuse and Mental Health Services Administration's National Survey on Drug Use and Health reported that the percentage of Asian Americans aged 18–25 who reported serious mental health issues rose from 2.9 percent to 5.6 percent between 2008 and 2018.[9]

Experiencing Racial Gaslighting

Asians who report microaggressions have historically been ignored. As a group, Asian Americans were not seen as a minority group that experienced racism, primarily because they are ingrained culturally to downplay frustrations for the greater good. The Chinese have even coined a term for this: "eating bitterness," known as "吃苦".

Victims of microaggressions are often further subjected to racial gaslighting, which is defined as manipulating the victims of a racial microaggression, second-guessing their validity, and causing the person to doubt their own experience. For instance, victims can be told, "Lighten up," "Don't be so sensitive," or "You must've misheard."

If you find yourself being racially gaslighted, it is best to seek outside support from friends and family, such as calling upon peers who can relate to and validate your experience, or find online Asian American communities to connect with. The nonprofit Stop AAPI Hate has also allowed AAPI to easily report hate incidents.

Learning Ways to Address Microaggressions

Growing up, I was frequently asked, "No, where are you really from?" Every time I was asked, I would initially freeze, because it was always so uncomfortable to know that, all of a sudden, I was being called out for looking physically different. I would usually just tell them what they wanted to know, which is where my parents are from. I never spoke up about how uncomfortable it made me feel; I just swallowed those feelings of being different. I know now that by not telling the person asking inappropriate questions, I didn't acknowledge that their actions were inappropriate, allowing them to continue this action with others.

You are not alone if you're on the receiving end of microaggressions; however, we have the opportunity to educate others along the way. The hope is that we can make the workplace better for ourselves and others by clearly addressing microaggressions. Psychologist Derald Wing Sue says, "Whether and how we respond to a microaggression is situational, but we don't have to passively let them happen to us or in front of us. There are ways, large and small, to push back and signal to both the perpetrator and onlookers that this is unacceptable behavior."[10]

How you react to someone is a reflection of who you are; how they react is a reflection of the reality they live in. Now that you understand the context of why microaggressions can be harmful, let's dive into how you can react to them. According to an article in the *Harvard Business Review*, "When and How to Respond to Microaggressions" by Ella F. Washington, Alison Hall Birch, and Laura Morgan Roberts, there are three main ways you can choose to react:[11]

- **Let it go:** Sometimes, you may not have the energy to deal with the microaggression, and it becomes emotionally draining to address it from the marginalized community receiving them.
- **Respond immediately:** This approach invites you to address the impact of the negative comment and explain the situation when it is fresh in the minds of everyone involved.
- **Respond later:** You may need time to digest what happened and decide to address the perpetrator privately to explain why it was offensive. You can even start off with, "I know you didn't mean it, but your comment was offensive because _____" and fill in the blank with why you feel that way.

You can learn to address microaggressions with the three Ds—direct communication, discussion, and dismantlement—to move the conversation forward when you experience microaggressions.

Using Direct Communication

Microaggressions are often subtle everyday interactions that convey bias toward a marginalized group; they are offensive to the person receiving them. With direct communication, you clearly let the aggressor know that what they said is harmful. To educate them, clarify what was offensive in their language and let them know that it is not okay to say what they said to you. Direct communication is recommended for a first-time offense from a stranger.

Using Discussion

If you know the microaggressor well, you might want to have an open discussion about why their language was hurtful. For instance, my friend's son was a toddler and she told me her son was "speaking like a Chinaman," a common phrase in the United Kingdom. However, I found it very offensive, because the message behind the saying is that Chinese people do not speak well. We had an open discussion where I made it clear that it is hurtful to describe speech this way. She was receptive to understanding and improving the way she communicates moving forward. Discussion is recommended for offenses from family or friends.

Using Dismantlement

You may often come across a repeat offender, and we encourage you to dismantle and break down why what they are saying is inappropriate. For instance, I had a manager who would often imitate our Korean client; he would use an Asian accent and squint his eyes while repeating the client's email responses. To address the microaggression, you can let the offender know it is offensive to mock someone's accent because it enforces prejudice, racism, and classism. To squint your eyes to depict Asians as a racist stereotype. It is essential to break apart why their actions are hurtful.

Intervening as a Bystander

As you continue to work with others, you may witness microaggressions occurring to other people. This is where you can intervene proactively as a bystander to support them. You can customize your approach depending on the situation, target the behavior more than the person, circle back in a more private setting, or seek outside support. Sometimes, a microaggression is unintentional, and a bystander can educate the perpetrator to encourage an honest conversation about the microaggression. You will learn more about interventions later in this book.

Interview with Jason Ve

Jason Ve is a tech, media, and music industry executive, speaker, and investor with over 15 years of experience at leading corporations and start-ups including Google, Disney, and Viacom. He advises, consults, and invests in start-ups and is a venture partner at Gaingels, the largest investment syndicate and network of LGBTQ+ investors. Jason serves on the board of directors of Asian Americans Advancing Justice (AAJC), a national nonprofit dedicated to advocacy for Asian Americans. He went to New York University's Stern School of Business.

What made you go down your current career path?

A pivotal moment of my career was actually my *American Idol* audition. My first job in the corporate world was investment banking on Wall Street, and I told my manager at the time that the *American Idol* auditions were in town and I was going to give it my best shot. I told my team that if I made it, they wouldn't see me back at my desk. Unfortunately, I was back at my desk the next day. However, my rejection at the auditions made me realize how incredibly passionate I was about music—as I showed up to the audition pretty frightened, having never auditioned for anything before. I set my goals on merging that passion for music with my knack for business. That fueled my decision to leave Wall Street and pursue a career in the entertainment and music business, and that has been my journey ever since. Trust and listen to that voice inside of you, try to figure out what drives you and what you're most passionate about. This will ultimately navigate you in the right direction.

Can you share an example of when you experienced microaggressions and what you did about it?

Growing up on gay dating apps, I would see two words in people's public profiles: "No Asians." The sick thing of it all was I saw it so much that I thought that this was just sort of normal, accepting it as a fact of being a minority living in America. I never initially processed it as a microaggression, nor the macroaggression that it is. Perhaps it was just my way of rationalizing it to get through daily life—getting through people's attempt at rendering my race invisible. But as I grew older, I realized how awful, unacceptable, and downright shameful that was. The events of the past few years were a necessary reset of important conversations that were long overdue in America.

Only recently have I muscled up the courage to speak up, stand up, and really think about the power of banding together and sharing our individual stories. In the past year I published an op-ed about my experiences growing up gay and Asian and called it "No Asians" (https://www.menshealth.com/trending-news/a36555932/jason-ve-confronting-no-asians/) to call out exactly those two words that I had seen all those years but felt powerless over. I now feel empowered to reclaim my power, reclaim my being Asian American and all the great that comes with that, and be proud to display my family's history. I have a responsibility for sharing my story and have made it a point to call out racism and microaggressions where I can (where it feels safe to do so), and to no longer stay as my traditionally-silent self as I thought I was supposed to be. I use these as education moments for the perpetrators, so that our society can learn to do better, for the Asian kids of today and tomorrow that cannot and will not go through what I and my generation of gay Asians went through. We deserve better than that.

How do you help those impacted by microaggressions?

If you see a microaggression happen, you could enter the situation and ask the aggressor to clarify, "What did you mean by that?" Or you can also choose to let the situation diffuse, and then check in with the person affected about how they feel. Checking in with the person that received the microaggression can go a long way when one witnesses it. It's important where we can to make sure the person affected feels supported, as chances are they feel really uncomfortable at the moment and negatively impacted by the microaggression that had just occurred.

I believe there's a uniqueness to being Asian, in that we may rationalize the situation as the subject of a micro- or macro-aggression, like I did, to internally make it a "non-issue". But I think it's important to find your own outlet for how you need to address it. You can directly confront the aggressor to state how that made you feel and state why it was inappropriate. It's also okay to not say anything if you don't feel comfortable, but find an outlet to discuss the situation - it could be with a trusted friend, a partner, or a colleague in your employee resource group. Another resource I'd recommend is Asian Americans Advancing Justice's free bystander intervention training, which goes through how to recognize microaggressions and tips on navigating through them when they happen to you or others around you.

How has being Asian affected your career?

Navigating my career in primarily white-dominated spaces initially made me feel like I should try to aspire to act like or be white. I wouldn't necessarily bring in my Asian identity and the customs I have at home at work or to my peers, unless it was "relevant" to the conversation or convenient. Only in more recent years have I realized the power of my identity and the uniqueness and richness of the experiences that it brings. I am my family's history, my own lived experiences, an Asian American, an LGBTQ+ citizen, and all of these things give me a unique perspective in and contribution to work and life. I've never been more proud to be all the particular aspects of me that have brought me to where I am today. And

I can't truly move forward if I don't take the rest of my community with me. I want to continue to propel Asian Americans and other diverse communities to feel represented at work, on the screen, and on the airwaves so that we collectively all feel seen, heard, and truly reflected in the fabric of our society.

It's an extremely powerful thing to be Asian at this current moment; we're living in a unique part of history with much more visibility than in years past. Do what feels natural or right to you in this moment; it might be a big thing you feel empowered to do or say, as you feel people may finally listen (go for it!). Or you might not want to do anything much different than before (that's okay too). But one thing's for certain—there's no longer a need to suppress or silence ourselves. That is so last decade.

Key Takeaways

- A microaggression is a comment or action that subtly and often unconsciously or unintentionally expresses a prejudiced attitude toward a member of a marginalized group, such as a racial minority.
- There are three ways to deal with microaggressions:
  o **Direct communication:** Point out the underlying message of the microaggression.
  o **Discussion:** If you know the microaggressor, have an open conversation to explain why the offensive language was hurtful.
  o **Dismantlement:** Break down why the microaggression is inappropriate, especially if the offense is a repeated one.

- Microaggressions can be harmful as they identify Asians as foreigners, affect the safety of the Asian community, and increase the stress levels for Asian Americans experiencing them.
- To effectively intervene as a bystander to address microaggressions, customize your approach depending on the situation, target the behavior more than the person, circle back in a more private setting, or seek outside support.

Reflections

- **How have you navigated past microaggressions?**
  o Write down three to five instances in which you experienced or witnessed microaggressions.
  o Then write which of the three Ds could have been best used to solve each situation. If you had a do-over, what would you have said in the moment?
- **How are you responding to microaggressions?**
  o Download the microaggression toolkit at: https://www .inclusiveatwork.com/micro, which includes ways to respond to microaggressions: restate/paraphrase, ask for clarification, acknowledge the feelings behind the statement, separate intent from impact, express your feelings, challenge the stereotype, promote empathy, and appeal to values.
  o Kevin Nadal, a professor of psychology at John Jay College, suggests asking yourself five questions when weighing the consequences of responding to microaggressions:

- If I respond, could my physical safety be in danger?
- If I respond, will the person become defensive and will this lead to an argument?
- If I respond, how will this affect my relationship with this person?
- If I don't respond, will I regret not saying something?
- If I don't respond, does that convey that I accept the behavior or statement?[12]

8

Maximizing the Power of Networking

Jessalin Lam

When I was first starting out in the industry, I had an exercise for myself where I would try to go out to a new event once a week and meet three new people. It wasn't about meeting everyone, it was about trying to intently get to know a few people more intimately with intention. The point being—get to know the human first and the rest will follow.

—Dan Matthews, managing partner and creative
producer at International Secret Agents

DO YOU GET nervous when you have to connect with new people at a networking event? Or you are not sure what questions to ask when trying to approach people for professional relationships? How do you follow up after you meet someone to nurture the connection? It's okay to not know where to start, and this chapter will help meet you where you are to equip you with how to learn and apply the skills of networking to benefit your career. I started networking when I was in college, and I remember I used to think it was weird to strike up a conversation with a random person, but networking is a skill that anyone has the capacity to learn as long as you take the time to practice and prioritize it.

As Asians, we know that it is not always culturally acceptable to ask those we don't know for help; however, forging connections and building bridges are essential for upward mobility. This chapter will guide you to discover the power of networking and unlock keys to help you connect with others and foster strong relationships in your own network. It will teach you how to reach out and nurture meaningful connections and will show you examples of how to craft thoughtful conversation starters. The chapter will uncover hindering cultural barriers and share real stories on how networking can open doors for your career.

Learning the Benefits of Networking

Let's start with what networking really is. *Business networking* is the process of meeting others to exchange information, make new professional contacts, and create helpful relationships. As Sallie Krawcheck, CEO and co-founder of Ellevest, a digital financial advisor, says, "The number one unwritten rule of success is networking."[1] This is why it is crucial for you to learn this skill. Knowing that 70 percent of all jobs are not published publicly on job sites and 80 percent of jobs are filled through personal and professional connections, you need to make sure you are meeting with the right people for opportunities that align with your goals.[2] These relationships are useful when you are looking for a new job, developing your skills, or increasing your industry knowledge. You can strengthen your networking skills like a muscle—the more you work on it, the better and stronger you will become at it.

When you invest your time in networking, you will learn that there are mutual benefits for creating long-lasting relationships with people you know. People with strong social networks tend to be more confident, happier, and healthier. According to *Forbes*, networking has many benefits.[3] Networking:

- Creates an avenue to exchange ideas;
- Increases your visibility for your career;
- Opens the door for new opportunities;
- Evaluates your qualifications for future roles;
- Builds your own resource library;
- Improves your growth and self-confidence;
- Develops long-lasting relationships;
- Introduces you to new connections.

It may surprise you to know that, even with all these benefits, only 25 percent of professionals actually network and 41 percent of them would like to network more but don't have enough time.[4] By learning to network successfully, you will position yourself ahead of the curve.

Unlearning Asian Cultural Barriers to Networking

Differences between Asian and Western culture need to be recognized and acknowledged as they affect how people within those cultures network. According to board-certified psychiatrist Dr. David Mee-Lee, cultural beliefs and norms are often unspoken and ingrained into our total being; we often don't even realize that we are holding onto them. In Asian culture, we may often think problems need to be accepted, not talked about. Many Asians believe it is best to keep secrets, to not express emotions, and to choose silence over discussion. Western culture, by contrast, focuses on proactively solving problems, talking about them, encouraging people to be honest and transparent, welcoming the expression of emotions, and valuing freedom of speech.[5]

When I facilitated a workshop for Asians in Advertising on how to network with ease, I heard many Asian American attendees identify cultural barriers as obstacles to networking. Some of the obstacles included:

- Feelings of bothering people when asking for a favor;
- Anxiety to start a conversation;
- Imposter syndrome;
- Being a burden to other people;
- Being uncomfortable advocating for themselves;
- Not knowing anyone in the industry;
- Being humble about accomplishments;
- Not having anything to offer;
- Being intimidated by senior people.

Now that you can see some of the obstacles, let's dive into ways for you to unlearn these cultural barriers to improve your networking skills.

Sharing Your Challenges and Goals

Asians are culturally uncomfortable talking about themselves and would rather appear to be humble. But this reticence to communicate about the problems they are facing and sharing them openly with people in their network only hinders their career development. If you feel this way, you will be delightfully surprised how people are willing to help and support you or share resources on how to solve the challenges you may be working through. Be strategic about who you share your challenges with. Experiment with your existing network or with new people you meet.

Example: You are at a business lunch catching up with someone in your network who is asking you how your new job is going. You share the challenge that you may feel like you are not learning as much as you would like to in your new role. You ask your contact to keep you top of mind for new job opportunities that would challenge you and utilize your full potential.

Being Honest and Transparent

Asians are brought up thinking that they do not want to be a burden to others, so being transparent can be challenging as they are used to pretending everything is okay rather than openly sharing problems with other people. When you communicate with anyone in your network, stay true and authentic to who you are. Vulnerability is even welcome when you connect with people as you share your story and personal experiences. It is always best to be honest and transparent as you want to make sure you are genuine in how you are presenting yourself. Don't forget to utilize the tools you learned when building your personal brand. You can apply them here as you use your voice when speaking with others.

Example: When you begin to build more connections in your network, people may poach you for new job opportunities. You can utilize this as leverage, especially if you are not actively seeking a new job, by being honest about what you are looking for. You may be a working parent looking for flexibility in a job to work remotely or you may be looking for a specific salary and compensation package that you view as nonnegotiable. In these kinds of inter-actions, you can apply the skills you learned in the chapter about knowing your worth.

Inviting Yourself to Take Up Space

You may be intimidated by others you perceive as successful or think you have nothing to offer to people in your network. Reframe the way you perceive yourself and know that you deserve to be where you are. Don't be afraid to take up space and shine when connecting with people. Don't be afraid of someone based on their job title when you are in the same room during a business networking event or meeting. You have a wealth of knowledge and experience that you bring to the table, and we invite you to take up space when you enter a room. You do not want to be a wallflower when there are opportunities waiting for you. If you do not speak up, people will have no idea who you are or what your perspectives or ideas are.

Example: You are in a meeting and decide to share an idea that will bring in new business to the organization and you are creating an opportunity for yourself to lead this new project based on your expertise to shape out the idea. This will not only increase your visibility, you will also be positively affecting the bottom line of the business to result in a win-win situation. Do not be afraid to voice your thoughts and suggestions to be seen and heard.

Improving Your Communication Skills

Some people may have anxiety when connecting with others. Remember that networking is a skill you can learn and get better at, especially when you work on improving how you communicate with people. Communication skills are critical to unlocking unlimited opportunities as they allow you to exchange ideas with other people as you continue to network. There is always room to improve how you communicate with someone, whether that is verbal, nonverbal, written, or visual. Here are communication types and ways to use them:[6]

- **Verbal**: practice strong, confident voice, avoid filler words, avoid jargon;
- **Nonverbal**: Acknowledge your body language, notice your emotions for how you express yourself;
- **Visual**: Consider your audience, use visuals to add value;
- **Written**: Use simplicity, keep records of effective writing to reference.

Example: You meet someone at a networking event and use effective communication with your elevator pitch about your dream job in the future. The point of contact you are speaking to sees you light up with your nonverbal communication for the passion you have, and they offer to introduce you to a point of contact for a virtual coffee with them. This is where you exercise your written communication to send a thank-you email with the call to action included to follow up on the opportunity.

Growing Your Network

Let's talk about how to grow your network. Where do you even begin? With whom do you talk? Networking is more about farming than it is about hunting. It's about cultivating relationships. For Asians, we know it may be uncomfortable to ask those we don't know for help, but remember that these connections will ultimately support your goals and career, especially those related to upward mobility.

As you think about growing your network, you should be aware of the different types of networks available to you: operational, personal, and strategic.[7]

- **Operational:** Gaining contacts in roles central to business success (executives, distributors, clients);
- **Personal:** Socializing with people who offer referral, knowledge, and support (references, coaches, mentors, friends);
- **Strategic:** Strategically seeking people you admire to connect with to share ideas (peers, industry leaders, and everyone in between).

Within each of these networks, you will need to identify the types of people you want to invest in. Every network will include the following kinds of people:

- **Mentors:** People who act like a sounding board and who share pivotal career advice;
- **Sponsors:** People who create opportunities for you to succeed;
- **Advocates:** People who mention your name when you're not in the room and have your best interests at heart;
- **Cheerleaders:** People who champion you and keep you motivated as you work toward accomplishing your goals;
- **Connectors:** People who connect you to people in their network.

Creating Your Own Networking Toolkit

We hope the tips in this chapter help make networking less intimidating to you, especially when you might not know where to start. Here are some suggestions to add to your own networking toolkit.

Knowing Where to Connect with People

You can connect with people in many ways beyond a cold outreach via email, which is unlikely to be successful. Here are some strategies for how you can source your new connections:

- **Following potential connections on social media:** Connect with people on LinkedIn, Twitter, and Instagram to follow their content. This is the best way to see what kind of content they share and then engage with them.
- **Attending speaking events:** Engage and register for events featuring the person you want to connect with to be strategic in listening to their insights. An example of a success story is when my mentee took my advice to attend an industry webinar, sent a note to one of the speakers requesting to connect, and landed an internship with them after letting them know what she was looking for. It is important to be intentional and proactive with the people you choose to connect with.
- **Reading (or listening to) potential connections' books, articles, and podcasts:** Stay up-to-date with the people who are writing articles and books, features in resources, or podcasts that are of interest to you. This is a great way to mention what you learned from them when you reach out to share your insights.
- **Joining industry organizations or communities:** Connect with people in similar fields by joining industry organizations or communities where you can look for volunteer opportunities that would expand your network.

- **Being active in your alumni association:** Your college will have an alumni association that you can tap into for a network of people either in the same industry as you or in industries you are looking to pivot to. You can ask your college how to connect with them.

These are only a few examples of how to connect with people. Try to think of creative ways to stand out as you reach out to new contacts.

Getting Started with the Initial Outreach

Now that you know who you want to connect with, how do you do your initial outreach? Here's our recommendation of what to include in your initial outreach via written communication after you met them. This will be a more strategic way to connect with the person through email or LinkedIn message.

- **Name:** Make sure you get the person's name right. You would think this is simple to remember, but so many people spell names incorrectly or they copy/paste a template and use the wrong name when sending a message.
- **Source:** Share how you found them—whether you found them on your own or whether someone referred you to them.
- **Who you are:** Pitch who you are. Be brief!
- **Why:** Share *why* you are reaching out to this person.
- **Call to action (CTA):** Make sure you include a call to action for them to take—whether to schedule a call or set up a meeting with you.

Here is an example of a written communication you can use as an email template to connect to the person as an initial outreach.

Email Template	Sample Email
Hi [**Name**], [**Insert source of how you know them**]. I am currently [**Position**]. I wanted to reach out to [**share why you're reaching out**]. I would love to [**insert CTA**] if you're open to it. Cheers, [**Your name**]	Hi Sydney, *Congrats for being 2020 CLO of the Year from CLO Media. I am currently a Learning & Development Director and taking a CLO Accelerator course. I wanted to reach out to learn more about your career journey as I am an aspiring Chief Learning Officer. I would love to schedule a call with you if you're open to it.* Cheers to Learning, Jessalin Lam

Preparing Conversation Starters

After a contact responds and you schedule your first meeting, prepare conversation starters to know what you want to get out of the meeting with the new contact. In case you need some suggestions on what you could talk about, here are pointers to get you started:

- **Goals:** People love to hear where you want to be as it shows your ambition and vision for your future. Goals could be short or long term. Make sure to ask your contact what their goals are; being an active listener helps build a bond between the two of you.

- **Challenges:** Remember to share the problems or challenges you are having in a positive way and to ask for recommendations on how to tackle them. Ensure there is a mutual exchange with your contact by asking what challenges they may have in their role, company, or industry.
- **Resources:** Ask your contact for resources that you are looking for or share resources with them after you hear what their goals or challenges are.
- **Career journey:** People enjoy hearing about others' career journeys so be sure to share yours. Also ask about theirs to understand how they got to where they are today.
- **Common interests:** Do your homework by looking up your contact on LinkedIn and review their digital presence. You may be able to find that they went to the same college as you, share a similar hobby, or have a common interest that you can ask about when networking.
- **Industry news:** Be wise to keep up with industry trends and news to be able to share them when appropriate in conversation with connections. For example, the company they are working for could have been recently acquired or they might have won a new client, which has been announced publicly.

Nurturing the Relationship

Let's say you now had the first meeting with your new connection or you met them at an event. The next step is to follow up and nurture the relationship to keep them in your network and to be top of mind. Here are some examples of how you could do this:

- **Be a giver:** Think about how you could help this person with their goals or share an opportunity they could benefit from. For example, there may be a scholarship or fellowship for which they qualify, and you could share that information with them.
- **Be thoughtful:** Remember things about the contacts you want to stay in touch with. Let them know you are thinking about them from time to time. For example, LinkedIn has a notification that you can turn on to tell you when people's birthdays are; you can send them birthday greetings as one way to stay in touch. You would be surprised how much these little things matter; reaching out to contacts only when you want something is not a successful strategy.
- **Make time:** There may be people in your network you want to strategically catch up with more frequently, such as your mentors or industry peers. Prioritize your time and schedule monthly or quarterly catch-ups with these people. You could also email people to say you're in a career transition and would love to brainstorm with them on options.
- **Be a connector:** Your connections are like social currency; be careful who you exchange your contacts with. When you find synergy in people you think would benefit from each other, feel free to offer a connection.

Be creative in how you nurture relationships in your own network. Some fun examples we have seen include people creating origami cranes or hearts to include in hand-written thank-you notes, creating digital illustrations to thank someone, or sending thoughtful gifts for someone's birthday to show gratitude. Remember, networking is like growing your own garden; you must water it to create opportunities throughout your career.

Interview with Kenny Nguyen

Kenny Nguyen is chief executive officer and co-founder of ThreeSixtyEight, a creative agency whose mission is to challenge common thinking to create an uncommon future. Since its inception, the agency has helped underdogs advance their causes through uncommon interactive experiences. Before ThreeSixtyEight, Kenny co-founded Big Fish Presentations, a company that focused on ridding the world of boring presentations through high-quality presentation design, presentation coaching, and speech-writing. He advocates for Asian and Pacific Islander professionals looking to find their voice in leadership.

What networking tips can you share with our community?

Drive a FORD EPIC! Great networking is understanding how to break open conversations that are memorable. To be a good conversationalist, you must ask great questions. For networking, understanding how to speak to others about their FORD—a person's Family, Occupation, Recreation, and Dreams—can help break the ice for convos. But these tend to be convo starters. So how can your conversation be even more memorable? I've found that EPIC—the acronym from the Heath Brothers' *The Power of Moments*—takes convos to a more intimate and vulnerable level as these are questions folks don't get asked frequently. EPIC stands for moments that the person feels Elevated, Prideful, Insightful, or Connected. You want to save these questions when you go deeper on a subject. Here are some examples:

- **Elevated** = "Can you tell me more about what stood out when you experienced X?" I find this question works best when you want to hear more about a story that sounds interesting.
- **Prideful** = "Can you tell me more about what made you so proud when you accomplished or overcame X?" I find this question works best after talking about a prideful moment that doesn't get enough recognition but should.
- **Insightful** = "Can you tell me more about what you learned after experiencing X?" I find this question works best when speaking about a life-changing experience.
- **Connection** = "Can you tell me more about what sticks out in your relationship with X?" I find this question works better when you are talking about a mutual friend or they know someone you admire.

So, if you want to start a convo, drive a basic FORD. If you're going to go deep, upgrade to an EPIC.

Can you share an example of how networking created an opportunity for you?

This question is difficult to answer because there are too many stories. I didn't finish college, so I don't have the university networks others have. I didn't start my career in advertising, so I knew no one in that field (clients included) when I started my business. What I did have, though, was genuine curiosity and a willingness to help people solve their problems (whether it was through me or through someone I knew). Being genuinely interested in helping others has led me to new clients, mentors, and life-long friends.

What resources do you recommend for networking?

I love Lunch Club. It's an AI platform that helps you virtually meet new people weekly in your targeted fields of interest. It's an extra plus that it's 1-1 and less exhausting than being in a giant chat room.

What are ways you continue to nurture relationships in your network?

Creating genuine relationships is essential. If you don't know where to start, try adopting your version of the RAIL acronym below:

- **R** stands for *referring*. Refer whomever you're speaking with to a new person, product, or service that can make their life better. People want to be around connectors that aren't just in it for themselves.
- **A** stands for *annoy*. Keep in touch often, but do so with a servant's heart. Instead of asking, "How can I help?" actually be intentional and offer something that adds value reflecting your last conversation together.
- **I** stands for *inform*. No matter if you may lose an opportunity to do business right away, help keep your audience informed with the right things they need to make a decision—even if they may not pick you for a project. People today want to be served, not sold.
- **L** stands for *love*. It's just as important to say "yes" to the right things as it's important to say "no" to the wrong things. People will respect your integrity and honesty if what they ask isn't in your wheelhouse.

How has being Asian affected your career?

It's made me realize three things:

1. That the barriers I break are not just for myself but others. It's important to share the lessons and not remain silent.
2. It's caused me to lose my voice because I was afraid of speaking out and always told myself, "When I have X, I will speak out." I learned that this is flawed thinking and that courage must start now. The more success I find, the more tempted I will be to keep the peace. Why wait?
3. It's given me a voice that carries weight when I speak out. During the beginning of the AAPI violence attacks, people were shocked the tragedies impacted me, as they never looked at me as someone that identifies as AAPI. Using my talent to turn complex messages simple through presentations and communications, I can get people who don't look like me to relate to the internal pain.

Key Takeaways

- Creating connections and building bridges are essential for upward mobility.
- 70 percent of all jobs are not posted publicly and 80 percent are filled through networking.
- To unlearn Asian cultural barriers to networking, you can share your challenges and goals, be honest and transparent, invite yourself to take up space, and improve your communication skills.
- The type of people to invest in as a starting point for your network include mentors, sponsors, advocates, cheerleaders, and connectors.
- Examples of where to connect with new people are social media, speaking events, books, articles, podcasts, industry organizations or communities, and your alumni association.

Reflections

- **Assess the type of networks you currently have as you look to grow your network.**
  o Dedicate a few hours each week to add one to three additional contacts across your operational, personal, and strategic networks. Track your outreaches on an Excel spreadsheet and include who you reached out to, the date, and if you heard back from them.
- **When you think about growing your network, what type of person do you need to invest in?**
  o Learn the difference between sponsorship and mentorship and the ABCs of sponsorship at: https://hbr .org/2021/06/dont-just-mentor-women-and-people-of-color-sponsor-them.
- **Think about additional ways you can network with new people.**
  o Try networking apps like Shapr Networking (https:// shapr.co/en-networking), lunchclub(https://lunchclub .com), BumbleBizz (https://bumble.com/en/bizz), or Fishbowl (https://www.fishbowlapp.com).
- **Consider more conversation starters you can include when connecting with new people.**
  o Pick a few from these 150 helpful conversation starters for networking professionals: https://www.indeed.com/ career-advice/career-development/conversations-starters. They can be used at corporate events, conferences, networking events, casual events, between employees, professional gatherings, and interviews.
  o Refer to additional networking convo starters from The Muse: https://www.themuse.com/advice/30-brilliant-networking-conversation-starters.

9

Becoming an Effective Leader and Manager

Bernice Chao

If you want to win in the 21st century, you have to empower others, making sure other people are better than you. Then you will be successful.

—Jack Ma, Chinese business magnate, investor, and
philanthropist

IN A CONVERSATION with Senna Bayasgalan, the director of marketing at Cordia, I learned about a concept that she learned in Korea called "nunchi 눈치," which is the subtle art and ability to listen and gauge other people's moods. It can be described as emotional intelligence. Senna realized that this was seriously lacking in the American workplace. She took it upon herself to use this concept in her own interactions with her team. As an example, when she worked in America, she was hired to create a new marketing team and had to expand the team. She noticed that a current team member was having a very adverse reaction to a new hire, so she took her to lunch and asked her how she was feeling about the new hire. The team member shared that she was insecure because she wasn't as educated as the new hire and felt her job was at risk. This conversation helped Senna understand where this employee was coming from. Senna shared her own personal story about feeling insecure about coming into a career that wasn't from her educational background. Having that moment of shared vulnerability made the team member feel like they had a trusted ally and ultimately made the team stronger.

This chapter addresses ways that Asians can be effective leaders in the American workplace—learning different management styles, tapping into authentic leadership, being vulnerable, and being positively assertive. Management styles can change depending on the type of company, management level, industry, and people. Those who are most effective have flexible management styles that can be adjusted based on different factors while still focusing on achieving goals.

For Asians, the ascent to a managerial position is often slower than most due to Asian stereotyping. While business leaders are often expected to be competent, intelligent, and dedicated, they are also likely to be charismatic and socially skilled—along with masculine and dictatorial or authoritarian. This puts Asian Americans at a disadvantage; they most often occupy low- to mid-level management positions, but not top-level leadership. A highly cited 2015 report on diversity in Silicon Valley by an Asian professional organization found that at five big tech firms (Google, Hewlett-Packard, Intel, LinkedIn, and Yahoo), Asians and Asian Americans are well represented in lower-level positions but underrepresented at management and executive levels.

It's even harder for Asian women—they comprise only 3.1 percent of executives in the five tech companies mentioned above, while Asian men comprise 13.5 percent.[1] The Equal Employment Opportunity Commission's (EEOC) workforce data found that Asian American white-collar professionals are the least likely group to be promoted from individual contributor roles into management—less likely than any other race, including Blacks and Hispanics.[2] These data points emphasize how scarce Asian managers are.

One of the most important jobs for companies is identifying the right managers, and it's often someone in plain sight. Gallup finds that companies fail to choose the candidate with the right talent for the job 82 percent of the time. Bad managers cost businesses billions of dollars each year, and having too many of them can bring down a company.[3] It is therefore critical that companies tap the right talent for leadership roles, and Asian Americans should become a larger presence in those roles.

Defining Managers versus Leaders

As you are managing others, it is important to understand the difference between managers and leaders. *Managers* use power and control to ensure goals are accomplished; managers are seen as administrators. On the other hand, *leaders* are people with the ability to influence, inspire, and motivate others toward success. Leadership is about creating an environment that allows people to opt into the vision, whereas management controls the processes.

You do not have to be managing others to be a leader. To deduce whether you are a leader, count the number of people that report to you versus the number of people that come to you for advice. If you have many people coming to you for advice, you're perceived as a leader. Being a great leader can have lasting effects on others outside of the group in achieving goals. For me, I started seeing the shift from just a mere manager to a leader when several non-reports at my workplace would contact me to talk about their careers. As I became more visible in the workplace as a manager, I transitioned into becoming a leader.

Understanding the Three Types of Leadership Styles

In 1939 Kurt Lewin, a German American psychologist known as one of the modern pioneers of social, organizational, and applied psychology in the United States, identified three types of leadership style: authoritarian, participative, and delegative. Each of these styles is distinct and has its own pros and cons.

> **Authoritarian:** This is the most restrictive of the leadership styles. It follows a top-down, one-way approach with employees. The manager makes all the decisions based on their expertise or power. Employees are micromanaged and are not encouraged to ask questions or contribute ideas.
>
> ■ **When to use this style:** This style is best used in times of crisis or when deadlines are tight. In these moments, the team needs a decisive leader to move quickly and be productive; however, it's best to switch styles after the crisis has passed.

- **Pros:** Managers can make quick decisions, and the team has clearly defined roles and expectations. The team is highly productive, and there are fewer misunderstandings.
- **Cons:** The authoritative management style doesn't allow the team to participate in asking questions. Because the team is treated as drones, work output will be less creative. A team that isn't heard typically feels less valued, increasing dissatisfaction and turnover.

Participative: This style is all about encouraging the sharing of ideas within the team. All team members have an active voice and are encouraged to participate in the discussion.

- **When to use this style:** Overall, this is considered the most effective day-to-day style to use in the workplace. This style allows the group to feel ownership in decision-making and valued as a team.
- **Pros:** This style facilitates team unity. Employees feel like they have a valued voice, contributing to the success of the business.
- **Cons:** This style is not particularly effective when quick decisions are needed. Employees may not feel comfortable participating in discussions in public settings.

Delegative: This is the hands-off management style. Delegative managers assign tasks and perhaps a general direction but are not involved in day-to-day tasks. Employees are tasked to find the best approach to fulfill their responsibilities. This method puts a lot of pressure on employees to stay accountable, and the success of the team is based on each individual's performance.

- **When to use this style:** This style is best if you have a highly proficient individual who can work without supervision.
- **Pro:** This method allows employees to feel the freedom to perform their tasks autonomously and gives those who are highly skilled and self-motivated a chance to make their job their own.
- **Con:** The lack of leadership oversight can lead to a loss of productivity or missing key milestones. The team can lose interest in the project without a leader championing it.

Self-awareness is the most critical aspect in choosing a leadership style. Is there a leadership style that feels more right for you, the team, or the current situation? Know that your style can switch from time to time as well. Being an effective leader is knowing what leadership types exist and adapting them along the way.

Acknowledging Characteristics of a Great Leader

Think about a leader you admire and the characteristics they hold that make them a great leader. To practice these characteristics for yourself, you can tap into authenticity, vulnerability, and assertiveness. It does not matter what job title or role you have, you can find the leader within yourself to lead by example in the workplace. You can inspire the people around you across peers, executives, clients, and your network. The best leaders are not the ones who know how to do their job well; they are the ones that can influence and inspire others. Keep taking proactive steps to improve your leadership qualities and develop the leader within you.

Embracing Authentic Leadership

Authentic leadership is a term that has been around since the 1960s but became popular when Bill George published his book *Authentic Leadership* in 2003. This book explains authentic leadership as being you and making room for others, too. This type of leader is preferred by most because teams want leaders who can connect and understand them. Leaders with an authentic leadership style bring themselves to their job and participate fully and honestly in the workplace. Authentic leaders foster teams that believe they can get their authentic selves to the workplace. Organizations that encourage authentic behavior are more likely to have engaged, enthusiastic, motivated employees and psychologically safe cultures.

Here are the key characteristics of an authentic leader:

- **Self-awareness:** They recognize their abilities, strengths, weaknesses, and limitations and have high emotional intelligence (EQ) in understanding others' reactions.
- **Great listener:** They practice active listening to understand what their peers and subordinates are saying and offer a broad perspective.
- **Genuine, modest, and humble:** They are sincere, authentic, and not egotistical.
- **Empathetic:** They understand that their employees are humans. They are perceptive about their employees' challenges and needs and make decisions to support them.
- **Goal-oriented:** They are transparent about long-term goals and potential obstacles. The authentic leader shares these goals and allows others to engage in helping to accomplish them.

Embracing Vulnerability

For Asians, sharing vulnerabilities with others can be altogether taboo. Asians feel the need to save face, which means doing what you can to avoid having other people lose respect for you. To be an effective leader, however, you must reject that perspective. It is essential to share your vulnerabilities with your team, to help your team get to know you and to be inspired. For me, this was a huge mental switch, that letting your guard down invites people in, instead of being a poor reflection on you. As a leader, I share day-to-day vulnerabilities with my team to let them know I am human as well; sharing brings us closer together to find more ways to relate to one another. American researcher Brené Brown is famous for her TEDx talk "The Power of Vulnerability,"[4] where she says the more we put up walls, the more fearful and disconnected we become. Sharing personal stories is a powerful way for leaders to empower their teams.

Tiffany Rolfe, the global chief creative officer of R/GA, shared how she spent her day balancing her workload and the demands of motherhood in a women's group. She showed a complete 24-hour snapshot of a day in her life. In this presentation, she noted every hour she woke up and went to bed, each hour with an accompanying photograph. There were moments of levity when her kids showed up on Zoom. She documented all the meetings and late nights working after her kids fell asleep. It was refreshing to see an influential leader showing that she had a life outside of work and that it was okay to admit that the balance was tricky.

Here are some habits of people who embrace their vulnerability:[5]

- They give themselves permission to be themselves;
- They keep learning and having a growth mindset;

- They embrace their emotions and feelings;
- They expose themselves to new experiences;
- They stop worrying about what others think;
- They practice self-compassion.

Embracing Assertiveness

The value attached to assertiveness varies from culture to culture. While nonassertiveness may be positively viewed as steadiness in East Asian cultures, it can be negatively interpreted in American cultures as a lack of confidence, motivation, or conviction. Cultural sayings reflect this: the Japanese say, "The nail that sticks out gets hammered down" and the Chinese say, "The loudest duck gets shot." In the United States, we say, "The squeaky wheel gets the grease." As an Asian leader in a Western culture, it is essential that you learn how to be assertive.

An interesting study was conducted that compared assertiveness levels between two Asian cultures. Investigators researched the "bamboo ceiling," where Asians seem to be disproportionately underrepresented in leadership positions. They compared the two most significant Asian subgroups: East Asians and South Asians. Across nine studies (n = 11,030), East Asians were less likely than South Asians and whites to attain leadership positions. Cultural differences in assertiveness consistently explained the leadership attainment gap between East Asians and South Asians, but not by prejudice or motivation. These results suggest East Asians hit the bamboo ceiling because their low assertiveness is incongruent with American norms concerning how leaders should communicate. The bamboo ceiling is not an Asian issue but an issue of cultural fit.[6]

As an East Asian, I was never taught the power of assertiveness, but I have since learned that being assertive is an essential trait of good leaders. Today, when I share a marketing campaign with a client, I can confidently assert my opinions on why the work was presented and why they should buy a particularly creative idea. I can also use my power of assertiveness to compel my team to achieve more.

Here are five ways to lead with positive assertiveness traits:

- **Connect and communicate:** Successful, assertive leaders do not "steamroll" others; instead, they connect with people at all levels of the organization and make themselves accessible. They take the time to communicate personally with individuals.
- **Provide honest feedback:** Assertive leaders provide good, honest, helpful, and fair feedback. The feedback delivered in the wrong way can be discouraging, demotivating, and even anger the employee. However, feedback that's offered with sensitivity can encourage those to try harder.
- **Have sound judgment:** Assertive leaders use their innate sense to be able to use good moral judgment when decision-making.
- **Maintain relationships:** An assertive leader who is well-liked, respected, and admired can exert influence and task others to perform complex tasks with less resistance than those who are disliked.
- **Create collaboration opportunities:** Assertive leaders resist the temptation to take on projects on their own for the glory; opening up to other groups usually allows a project to be more successful.

While you may feel that being assertive can feel inauthentic, it shouldn't. Being assertive should involve being friendly and positive. It can be part of your current style to the degree that feels appropriate for the working situation. Think of assertiveness as leading your team through difficult situations with confidence.

Interview with Prashanthi Raman

Prashanthi Raman has nearly 15 years of experience navigating challenging, highly charged, and complex political environments. As the vice president of global government affairs for Cruise, an all-electric, autonomous vehicle company, she oversees public policy and regulatory issues for the company worldwide. Before Cruise, Prashanthi served as head of state and local government relations at Lyft, where she played a pivotal role in creating and expanding the ridesharing industry across North America. In her spare time, Prashanthi serves on the board of the National Domestic Violence Hotline, PowHERful Foundation, and New Leaders Council. She is a graduate of Northwestern University and the Chicago-Kent College of Law and received her master's degree in public health from the University of Illinois at Chicago. Prashanthi resides in the Bay Area with her husband and two daughters.

What is your style of leadership?

I am empowering, transparent, and elevating. Oftentimes in my career, I felt as though I did not have enough context or was not able to own a workstream. I want individuals to know that we trust them and empowering them in their own role is just one way to do that. It is also very important for me to create a positive, encouraging, and psychologically safe environment for them to grow and succeed. I provide direct, firm yet kind feedback and always make sure to shout out the wins—from small to big!

What was the hardest part about transitioning into a leader?

It was honestly twofold: (1) believing I truly belonged in that "leader" category even though I knew somewhere I believed it. Impostor syndrome can really mess with you. (2) Knowing that I could no longer be in the working group if I was also going to approve the recommendation of the same group. Team members really wanted me to engage in the building of the recommendation and so I had to encourage them to try it by themselves first.

What advice would you give to others in becoming a leader?

Know your craft and surround yourself with others that complement your skill set. Learn from them and understand that becoming a leader is about taking ownership and thinking big.

What resources do you recommend?

A solid personal board of directors that knows you can advise you without judgment and can help chart out a path with you on where you want to go, Steven Covey's *The 7 Habits of Highly Effective People*, and the power of believing that you have the ability to make a change and a difference in this world.

Key Takeaways

- There are three types of leadership styles:
  - **Authoritarian:** The manager makes all the decisions, based on their expertise or the power they wield. Employees are micromanaged and are not encouraged to ask questions or contribute ideas.
  - **Participative:** This style is all about encouraging the sharing of ideas within the team. All members of the team have an active voice and are encouraged to participate in discussions.
  - **Delegative:** This is the least controlling management style. These managers will assign tasks and perhaps a general direction, but they are not involved in day-to-day tasks.
- A manager uses power and control, and a leader is more inspiring to influence and motivate others toward success.
- Authentic leaders are self-aware, great listeners, genuine, empathetic, and goal-oriented.
- Five ways to lead with positive assertiveness traits include connecting and communicating, providing honest feedback, having sound judgment, maintaining relationships, and creating collaboration opportunities.

Reflections

- **Consider your leadership style and where you may need to make adjustments for your employees.**
  - Review the pros and cons of the three leadership styles—authoritarian, participative, and delegative.
- **Identify a leader you find aspirational and learn from how they lead.**

o This can be someone in your company or someone you reach out to via LinkedIn.
- **Think about if you are a leader, a manager, or both.**
  o Hone your leadership and manager skills with these recommended books:
    - *The Making of a Manager* by Julie Zhuo;
    - *Crucial Conversations* by Joseph Grenny;
    - *How to Win Friends and Influence People* by Dale Carnegie.
- **Are there moments where you can be more vulnerable to your team?**
  o Read *No Hard Feelings: The Secret Power of Embracing Emotions at Work* by Liz Fosslien and Mollie West Duffy. Take their assessments focused on you, your team, and your organization to help you understand your emotional tendencies, your team's emotional culture, and your company's emotional norms.
- **What is your current leadership style like?**
  o Take the free Mind Tool assessment based on Kurt Lewin's Leadership Styles Framework: https://www.mindtools.com/pages/article/leadership-style-quiz.htm.

10

Optimizing the Magic of Mentorship

Bernice Chao

Understand that one day you will have the power to make a difference, so use it well.
　　　　　　—Mindy Kaling, American actress, comedian, writer,
　　　　　　　　　　　　　　　　　　　producer, and director

FIVE YEARS AGO, I worked with an intern named Houtan Sharafatian at an advertising agency called David & Goliath. Two years later, he reached out to me on LinkedIn with the message, "I remember always having really candid conversations with you, and was wondering if I could pick your brain about how I should proceed with pursuing jobs in marketing?"

When we connected, he wanted to talk to me about the next stage in his career and recalled the advice I had given him a few years earlier about creating a career path that mattered to him. He said how much he appreciated that

159

I stopped to have meaningful conversations and how they helped him navigate his career.

Last year he reached out to me again. "I know it's been a while since we last talked a while back, and I was asking you for some life advice. I was hoping to ask you for some help again if you have a chance to chat!" We talked about how he applied our last conversation to how he's currently navigating his career and wanted to talk about which classes to take during his MBA program at Loyola Marymount University. He also asked if I could help make an introduction to someone in my LinkedIn network for a job opportunity, which I was happy to do. After knowing more about what job he was looking at, I followed up with a few more jobs that I saw that he might also be interested in.

This is an example of how a mentee kept his connection warm with a mentor and let the mentor know that the time spent together was worthwhile. It's moments like these that are the best reminder of why mentorship and guidance are critical for career development and growth within our industry.

As an Asian American, I fully believe in the importance of mentoring and being a mentee within our community when possible. Sharing the same cultural background can help mentees navigate similar experiences, learn to tackle cultural challenges, and share strategies on the way. I have been able to share my positive and negative experiences in my work experiences, including those I have had as an Asian American. It has been invaluable to share my experiences with others who can relate to the same bias and barriers.

This chapter will teach you how to make the most of your time as a mentee as well as how to be an effective mentor, with tips and example questions for making the relationship meaningful.

Making the Most of Being a Mentee

Dora Li, a learning and development consultant at Wells Fargo, talks about how you can find a mentor in some surprising places. When Dora received the news that she was not selected for a job, she asked if there were skills she could develop and stretch projects she could work on to be a better candidate the next time a similar role became available. As a result, Cat Fischer, a senior business initiatives consultant, agreed to meet with Dora monthly to discuss the role in detail and give her long-term career guidance. Dora was able to turn an unfortunate situation into a career opportunity, showing that mentors can be found in unlikely places.

As a person ascending in your career, you can gain a lot of wisdom from someone who is further ahead in their career. Mentorship can help you see what your path ahead looks like, avoid some pitfalls, and help you advance in your career. When you have been paired with or identified with someone you would like to have as a mentor, make the most out of the mentorship. Mentors can be found within a school, organization, workplace, or interaction.

There are five ways you can maximize being a mentee:

1. **Own the calendar:** The best mentees that I've had are the ones who make sure we meet. Scheduling time is something for the two of you to discuss in your first meeting. Find a time that works, and if needed, set a recurring calendar invite.

2. **Be prepared:** Be clear about your needs and come with questions, topics, and goals you want to cover. You can track these conversations in a spreadsheet.

   Example discussion questions:

   - What was your career path?
   - What do you wish you knew earlier?
   - What was a rewarding project or experience?
   - How did you navigate a raise or promotion?
   - What are some recommended resources?
   - What skills do I need to move ahead?
   - How can I get better at presenting work?
   - How do you balance work and life?
   - How do you navigate weakness?
   - How do you manage up or down?

3. **Be open to feedback:** Your mentor is there to help you and to give you honest feedback. Keeping an open mind to ways to improve can help you refine your skill set and help you skip ahead in your career.

4. **Be action-oriented:** If your mentor gives you advice or actions that they recommend you take, do it. Ignoring feedback is showing your mentor that you do not appreciate their input. If you disagree with the feedback, it's okay to say so, but not acting on it otherwise is showing this person a lack of effort on your part. For example, if they provide you with feedback on how to clean up your résumé, you should take their advice and make those improvements. Or if they're sharing job postings, then apply. If they're making introductions to people in their network, follow up.

5. **Show gratitude:** Most likely, your mentor is a person who is very busy and making time to meet with you, so not only do you need to show up but you need to express

your thanks. You can extend your appreciation with a social media shout-out, LinkedIn recommendation, or sending a gift. A little extra goes a long way.

Being an Effective Mentor

Mentoring is beneficial and an incredible experience for the person being mentored, but it's also very rewarding for the person acting as the mentor. In general, not only are mentees promoted five times more than those without mentors, but amazingly, mentors themselves are six times more likely to be promoted over those who don't engage in mentorship.[1]

Here are five ways to mentor effectively:

1. **Make sure you're the right fit:** Figure out what the mentee's expectations are and ask yourself if you are the right person to help. It's helpful to find commonalities such as if your mentee is interested in your company, profession, cause, or shares a similar cultural background. Having commonalities is an important part of the mentorship program as it creates a bond and promotes respect between you and your mentee; beyond that, it will reaffirm the importance of the mentor program on both sides of the coin.

2. **Be a great listener:** Let your mentee speak. While we all feel like we have the knowledge to expound and wisdom to share, it's more important that you listen to your mentee's feelings and concerns.

3. **Engage:** It is essential to show up at each conversation with questions to make the time worthwhile. If you feel like your mentee needs time to prepare for the conversation, you can send them questions ahead of time.

Example discussion questions:

- What are things that bother you?
- What was a rough moment for you this week?
- What does success look like to you?
- Where are you looking to improve?
- Where do you see yourself in your career?
- What was a win you had this week?
- What do you love outside of work?
- What inspires you?
- What are your short- and long-term goals?
- What do you consider to be your strengths?

4. **Go with the flow:** Each relationship will be different, so find your own unique way to make the relationship meaningful. Perhaps you have a mentee who wants hard feedback or another one who needs more reassurance. As you work with your mentee, figure out the best way to steer the conversation so the information is communicated effectively.
5. **Help them forward:** This is the most important job as a mentor. It can take the form of sharing resources, recommending them for a job, or making introductions to others.

Using Different Types of Mentors

Surrounding yourself with a "dream team" of mentors can contribute significantly to your overall career success. Anthony Tjan, the CEO of the Boston venture capital firm Cue Ball Group and the author of *Good People*, recommends having five different types of mentors in your corner:

Mentor 1: Master of craft. This is someone who is the best in your field and can help you identify how to refine your craft.

Mentor 2: The champion of your cause. This person can be either at your workplace or in your field, but they're advocating for you and providing you with opportunities.

Mentor 3: The copilot. This person is someone you work with who understands what you're going through. Your copilot is someone you can strategize and collaborate with; you hold each other accountable.

Mentor 4: Your anchor. This person doesn't have to be in the industry. They can even be a friend or family member. This person keeps you grounded, consoles you, and is that voice of reason.

Mentor 5: The reverse mentor. This person is someone younger in your field or a mentee who can give you a fresh perspective and feedback on your leadership style.

The relationship with your mentor or mentee should be long-lasting and meaningful. You never know when you need advice, support, or a recommendation for a future job. Easy ways to stay in touch can include following them on social media and commenting on posts, sending a yearly email about what you have been up to, or arranging for an annual coffee. All relationships take effort to keep the connection warm.

Interview with Jerry Won

Jerry Won is a keynote speaker, workshop facilitator, and host who has worked with some of the world's most recognized brands in corporate and higher education. He speaks on a variety of topics including authentic storytelling, personal branding, the creator economy, and the Asian American experience in the workplace. He is the founder and chief executive officer of Just Like Media, an Asian American storytelling company whose award-winning podcast brands Dear Asian Americans, MBAsians, The Janchi Show, and Asian Podcast Network have partnered with McDonald's, Focus Features, and the US Census Bureau. Previously, he was a senior strategy consultant at Accenture and a sales leader at start-ups and Fortune 500 companies. Jerry has a Bachelor of Science from USC Marshall and an MBA from Michigan Ross, where he served as president of the Student Government Association. He currently serves on the Marshall Volunteer Leadership Council and the Michigan Ross Sanger Leadership Center Advisory Board. Along with his wife, Kyung, and his two children, Jerry lives in southern California.

Tell us about *Dear Asian Americans*.

Dear Asian Americans is a podcast show I created on March 2, 2020. This date is unique because it is my daughter's birthday. This entire project is dedicated to her and the kids of her generation so that we can leave them with Asian American stories that I didn't have growing up. So far, we've been regularly producing podcast episodes and recorded a hundred episodes in the first year. All of our interviews are anchored on the origin stories of how Asian people became Asian Americans. I think it's critically important to understand when, where, and under what circumstance we came to this country, whether through voluntary immigration, involuntary refugee, involuntary adoption, or other processes that made us Asian American. We try to be as representative as we can in the stories that we tell that also even break the stereotype of what an Asian American looks and sounds like.

How can Asian Americans pay it forward to the community?

Start by sharing your story. You can share it deliberately, as I do in my profession, or passively by sharing your experience on LinkedIn, Facebook, and Instagram. Stories are critically important because we live in a generation that has prioritized content creation. Still, a lot of content lacks context, the lens through which we see and absorb stories. For example, suppose somebody teaches you the top 10 ways to become a CEO. It doesn't matter if those rules are written by somebody who's not from your community; because we all battle different things, we have other avenues to success. There are a lot of cultural norms and that's something that we have to work through.

How can you be a good mentee?

Identify how you want to be helped. I need help with _____. What is your perspective on this _____? Be concise, precise, and respectful; follow up; and always maintain the relationship. You can also ask what you can do for that person because human psychology is funny. Once you ask somebody how you can help them, magically, they want to help you.

How can you be a good mentor?

Ask. I think we come up with all these rules on what a mentor is like, but we can start by simply asking the person we're helping. How do you want to be helped? What can I do? Because I can do a lot of things for you. Do you want me to make some phone calls for you? Do you want me to help you with your résumé? Like where are you stuck? If the person says they don't need any help, you can move on to the next person you can help.

How has cultivating meaningful relationships opened opportunities?

I have built long-lasting and meaningful connections, many for 10–20 years. Some of these connections were instrumental in helping me start my podcast, were brought on as a guest, introduced me to people, helped me find sponsors, and offered me paid speaking opportunities at companies. The marginal success that I've had with *Dear Asian Americans*, with speaking gigs, and recently an invitation to the White House has been a result of these meaningful connections.

Key Takeaways

- Mentorship is both beneficial to the mentor and the mentee.
- Mentors can come from a variety of places including school, workplace, organizations, and interactions.
- Being a good mentee, means being proactive at keeping the relationship active.
- A good mentor is someone who is not only a great listener but who also helps to push their mentee forward in their career.
- It's beneficial to have five different types of mentors: master of craft, champion, copilot, anchor, and reverse mentor.

Reflections

- **What would you like to gain as a mentee?**
  - o Identifying specific asks helps your mentor know how to most effectively help you in your career.

    For example:

    - Can you recommend me to _____ in your network? There's an opening at their office that I want to apply for.
    - Would you take a look at my résumé and give me some suggestions on how I can improve?
    - I'm applying for a new job; can I use you as a reference?

- **As a mentor are you being effective?**
  - o Here are recommended mentorship books:
    - *Mentoring 101: What Every Leader Needs to Know* by John C Maxwell;
    - *Learning to Lead: The Journey to Leading Yourself, Leading Others, and Leading an Organization* by Ron Williams;
    - *Helping People Change: Coaching with Compassion for Lifelong Learning and Growth* by Richard Boyatzis, Melvin Smith, and Ellen Van Oosten;
    - *Dare to Lead* by Brené Brown.

- **How can you build a diverse network of mentors?**
  - o Take a look at the TEDx Talk "Why Leadership and Mentorship Does Not Need to Fail Us" by Tony Tjan. https://www.youtube.com/watch?v=mibnG8XeHl U&t=37s

PART

III

Redefining the Future of the Workplace

11

Leveraging Allyship

Jessalin Lam

"Allyship is critical. Effective allyship is rooted in humanity. It must be authentic and intentional. It should never be passive tokenizing cheerleading. True allies defend, support, and empathize authentically for all people excluded from access to equity and equality."
— Ericka Riggs, chief diversity, equity, and inclusion officer,
Omnicom Specialty Marketing Group

WHAT EXACTLY IS allyship? According to the Center for Creative Leadership, "Allyship refers to the actions, behaviors, and practices that leaders take to support, amplify, and advocate with others, especially individuals who don't belong to the same social identity groups as themselves."[1] We all have different types of privileges that we may not often think of on a daily basis, including education, ability, language, income, race, or age. We can use that privilege to help others. It is incredibly powerful when we step up to be an ally for others.

This chapter will discuss how the Asian community can leverage allyship with other communities and how to get involved in employee resource groups if available at their company. The chapter also provides actionable tips on how anyone can be a better ally and how we can all work together to bring forth a better future.

Understanding Misconceptions about Allyship

Before we go into how to be an effective ally, consider the misunderstandings of allyship. When you better understand these misconceptions, it will help you become a better ally. The three common misconceptions about allyship are performative allyship, position, and perfection.[2]

Performative Allyship

Performative allyship is when people with privilege claim they are in solidarity with a cause, but it is only surface level where their actions are based on the idea of self-gratification rather than on the real desire to support the marginalized community. Many organizations or people may do this to protect their brand from being negatively highlighted. We do not want to see employers or leaders continuing empty gestures of saying they want to be an ally but not actually taking any action to support this or to stay accountable.

Position

You also need to remember that anyone can be any ally across any level or role, and it does not matter what title or position you have. Some people may think it is up to senior executives to make a change, but anyone can continuously put effort to educate themselves to do the deep work and make the marginalized group feel valued and safe without placing the burden on them.

Perfection

Fear of perfection holds back some leaders from becoming more effective leaders, and we are here to remind you that there is no perfect ally. You will never get it right every time, and it is key to give yourself grace as you keep learning. It is more about focusing on the intent and impact you have on others and doing what is right. This is why we encourage you to have the tough conversations and collaborations in order to create trust and psychological safety.

These misconceptions damage the racial equality agenda, and there needs to be more substance and long-term solutions that are sustainable when it comes to allyship. Stay engaged and be open to feedback to truly see the power of allyship.

Being an Effective Ally

Let's dive into how someone becomes an effective ally and what they do to make that happen. An ally will have an open mind to actively listen, be aware of implicit bias, do research to learn more about the history and struggle of the marginalized group, use their privilege to amplify suppressed voices, and do the work to become a better ally. It is crucial to be more intentional and understand actionable ways to be an ally. An effective ally takes an approach that is more proactive than reactive by building a strong foundation of competencies, knowledge, and awareness with a focus on other people, not yourself. Here are some ways to be a more effective and action-focused ally.

Speaking Out and Checking In

As a leader, acknowledge what is happening and check in with the community. Silence is complicit, and what is unsaid speaks volumes. You do not want to ignore what is happening in reality. Make sure you take the time to check in with people to ensure they feel safe, seen, and heard. You can simply say to an Asian colleague, "I see what's happening to the Asian community and it's not okay. Let me know if you want to talk about it." This will help them feel visible when you make it a priority to acknowledge what is happening in the news.

Educating Yourself

Be proactive by learning what else you can do, whether it be reading up on the history, taking an allyship and bystander training, or following leaders you could learn from. Effective allyship requires continuous learning about the communities you want to be an ally for. We recommend that you use all the free resources available to you before asking the marginalized community to teach you.

Amplifying Voices to Be Shared

Leaders can step up and create a safe space for employees as an ally by asking them for their perspectives. Be empathetic: ask them if they feel comfortable sharing their experience and listen to what they're sharing instead of waiting to respond with your own story. For those employees who are open to the idea of sharing their perspective more widely to the organization, amplify their voices to be heard and seen. For example, an employer can facilitate listening circles in safe spaces for people to open up about how they are feeling.

Calling Out Inappropriate Behavior

When you are an ally, you proactively show that you not only see and hear what is happening, but you also take the appropriate action to stand up for others. If you hear someone being disrespectful among your peers in the workplace, do the right thing to call out inappropriate behavior and prioritize psychological safety. You want to make sure the problem is addressed by saying directly that the disrespect is unacceptable, telling your human resources department, and checking in with the person who was on the receiving end.

Continuing to Move Toward Action

Allyship may start with awareness, move to education, and only then result in action. We encourage you to keep going. You are not aiming for perfection. It may be uncomfortable at times when being an ally for others, but this is how change is going to take place. Think about what you can do as you empathize with others.

Considering Ways to Leverage Allyship

Sometimes, you can leverage allyship to help a community with small steps and actions. For example, when I was exhausted, heartbroken, and lost for words during the rise of attacks on the Asian community across the United States, I expressed my concern casually to a colleague that

I was disappointed in leadership not addressing this and being silent. The next day, this colleague sent the staff an email about how the Black employee resource group stands in solidarity with the Asian community, encouraged people to donate to Stop AAPI Hate, and shared statistics and resources to educate people. My heart was so full; I was in tears of happiness to see that take place in the workplace. This colleague of mine not only heard my frustration but also took it upon himself to take action about it.

Embracing Intersectionality in the Workplace

Intersectionality is a term coined by law professor Kimberlé Crenshaw to describe the way people's social identities can overlap. As Crenshaw says, "Intersectionality is a lens through which you can see where power comes and collides, where it locks and intersects. It is the acknowledgement that everyone has their own unique experiences of discrimination and privilege."[3] Employers who welcome intersectionality in the workplace will create a sense of belonging for their employees to find commonalities and unlock shared humanity to see people as a whole person rather than focusing on visible differences. As a leader, we welcome you to embrace who you are with all your different layers and complexities including race, gender, age, sexuality, mental/physical ability, and nationality.

Getting Involved in Employee Resource Groups

Employee resource groups (ERGs) enable employees to have a community to connect with in the workplace with a shared characteristic or life experience. We encourage you to participate in your company's ERGs or create one if they do not exist. Consider joining as allies to other ERGs to learn from them and understand how you could support them. You can also create ways to collaborate, organize events, and share resources as you unite together for a larger impact.

Mentoring Marginalized Communities

In addition to looking for mentors or mentees, try to mentor people from marginalized communities to support their growth. You already learned about the magic of mentorship in a previous chapter. Mentor-mentee relationships are valuable as they help people reach their full potential.

Interview with George Sycip

George Sycip is a 10+ year veteran at Bloomberg, where he's held various positions in Supply Chain and now heads up the Engineering CFO Department's Business Analytics team. An immigrant from the Philippines, as well as an LGBTQ+ leader in both the company and the broader community, he holds an MBA from Columbia University and received a bachelor's degree in civil engineering from The Cooper Union for the Advancement of Science and Art. He lives in Bucks County, Pennsylvania, with his partner Scott Reed.

What actions can people take to be an effective ally for the Asian community?

Allyship is foundational to any meaningful impact in all social movements. Without allyship, we'd be advocating within an echo chamber of people within the community who already understand and experience the discrimination, hate, and inequity, unable to foster the change required for meaningful impact. Allyship is a spectrum and a journey based on understanding and authenticity. Being present, as in having friends, family, and colleagues in the community, is not allyship. Allyship is more than merely being present and saying you "support" them. "Active Allyship" is using your reach to advocate and fight for change.

As an ally, listen, learn, and research the inequities that the Asian community faces. Be prepared to be uncomfortable, as you will learn things that may make you uneasy. Rest assured that it's not going to hurt you. Settle into that discomfort.

- Meet and build authentic relationships with the community.
- Ask questions to understand examples of how the challenges have impacted their lives.
- Be intentional about listening to the details and be curious about people.
  o Consider how situations came to be. Did language, income, education, and social norms play a role?
  o Consider how your own levels of access may be different by being Asian, an immigrant, or simply different.
    • What school(s) did you attend?
    • Did both of your parents work? What did they do?
    • Did you have a large, supportive family?
    • Did you need to learn a new language?
    • Was money an issue?
- Forgive yourself. You will make mistakes, and it's okay.

The most profound way of showing allyship is by not being a passive bystander when you see microaggressions manifest in your day-to-day life. Bystander Intervention allows you to take active steps in addressing a situation that targets someone:

- **Direct**: Confront directly. By engaging in the moment, you give the person a chance to collect themselves or leave the situation
- **Distract**: Distract either party.
- **Delegate**: Involve someone else.
- **Delay**: Follow up with the person affected and provide emotional support or additional resources

Can you share an example of how you have leveraged allyship?

Building a Lesbian, Gay, Bisexual, Transgender, Queer + (LGBTQ+) Employee Resource Group (ERG) in our company was only possible with allyship. Doing this opened doors and enabled us to invite more people to partake in diversity, equity, and inclusion conversations that were occurring locally, nationally, and internationally. Going back to building authentic relationships, how does someone build if they don't know how to engage?

To set the stage, in 2011, marriage equality was a heated local and national debate. Same-sex marriage was a patchwork of laws, where some individual states permitted it, the same way other countries permit marriage. Unfortunately, the Defense of Marriage Act (DOMA), a federal law that become effective on September 21, 1996, prohibited the federal government from recognizing same-sex marriages. This blocked access to 1,100 federal rights and responsibilities associated with the IRS, social security, immigration, and family medical leave that come with "marriage." Most people know what marriage means, but the question was who had access to marriage.

To put this into perspective, Edie Windsor and Thea Spyer, a lesbian couple of more than 40 years were legally married in Toronto, Canada. Their marriage was recognized in New York State. When Thea died in 2009, her estate was granted to Edie with a federal estate tax bill of $363,000 from the IRS, which would not have been the case had DOMA not existed or if they were a straight married couple.

Consider that most local laws (and HR benefits) are written and passed by people who are not within the LGBTQ+ community. Allies are required to give a meaningful voice to advocate and enact change. Affording same-sex couples equal rights under the legal definition of "marriage," without any qualifiers was not law. Anything other than "marriage," such as "domestic partner," would not be equal, requiring each existing law to be modified in each jurisdiction within each state. At the time, this local social movement was the LGBTQ community's moment to build allyship amongst our friends, family, and colleagues to enable change. "Kitchen table" conversations around what marriage equality meant and why "domestic partnership" wasn't enough were common. Allies within the company helped update policies and HR benefits to help minimize the impact that could be directly tied to the gaps in marriage equality. Unfortunately, a company's jurisdiction is only so limited, and the issue was much broader. Fortunately, allyship at the local level helped enable the national political movement around marriage equality, which resulted in its expedient codification into federal law.

Forming the ERG gave our community a legitimized way to come together and be a resource. More importantly, it allows our colleagues to build authentic relationships, ask questions, and listen to the challenges in the community. These work colleagues then transitioned into allies and turned into advocates for our cause. We, along with hundreds of other companies, had an expanded voice in our advocacy to help the court support marriage equality, which we used to sign onto amicus briefs to the courts, sharing why these laws were hurtful or discriminatory. Read more at: https://www.bloomberg.com/news/articles/2015-03-05/from-goldman-to-google-companies-back-gay-marriage-in-supreme-court-brief#xj4y7vzkg?sref=V1DK3gxX

What resources do you recommend for people to learn how to become an ally?

The internet is the most effective and efficient resource we all have access to. Social media has made understanding issues easier and faster; it's no wonder TIME Magazine's "Person of the Year" in 2006 was "You" because of the content we all produce on social media. Follow influential people on Twitter, Instagram, Facebook, and TikTok. Once you've figured something out, use Google to research it a bit more, and tap into the community to see how you can support change. If you have access to an employee resource group, join it.

There are countless resources for becoming a better ally, but I think owning who you are and your experiences is the most authentic resource you have. Every family has its norms and challenges. Yours may be very similar to another with a different context altogether. Being humble enough to understand your own privilege and access (what you have without having to work for, i.e., laws that impact straight cisgender people or living in NYC) will help frame how you approach different communities and how you can relate with each other. Many communities have intersectionalities that are very similar, but can be viewed through different lenses.

For example, let's talk about our relationship with food and how it has become one of my most favorite ways of connecting with others. As a Filipino immigrant, my family ate at different times of the day. We shared a large stew and heated up lunch and dinner from the same pot throughout the day. The ingredients that went into that food came from various markets and were sometimes only relegated to the ethnic aisle in the grocery store.

I was embarrassed to bring my chicken and rice stew "baon" to school in the first grade. My family ate with their hands, something completely taboo in western culture. I would later find that, as an adult, food was a gateway to different parts of the world and should be celebrated. Inviting friends new and old to a Filipino Balicbayan night where food is spread on a long table atop banana leaves and everyone eats with their hands was an authentic exposure to our culture and lends itself to a deeper and more intimate understanding of how we socialize around food.

Filipinos are not alone in eating with their hands. Indian, Ethiopian, and Oaxacan cuisines are often enjoyed exclusively by hand. Food is just one authentic and fun pathway to connecting and finding intersectionalities with others.

Key Takeaways

- Allyship is the actions and behaviors that people take to amplify and advocate for others. As an ally, it is essential to acknowledge your privilege and support marginalized groups to create more inclusive environments.
- To be an effective ally, speak out and check in, educate yourself, amplify voices, call out inappropriate behavior, and continue to move toward action.
- You can leverage allyship with other communities by embracing intersectionality, getting involved in employee resource groups, and mentoring marginalized communities.

Reflections

- **What allyship actions are you using to show up for other communities?**
  - o Here is a list of 20+ allyship actions for Asians to show up for the Black community written by Michelle MiJung Kim: https://medium.com/awaken-blog/20-allyship-actions-for-asians-to-show-up-for-the-black-community-right-now-464e5689cf3e.
- **Educate yourself about Asian American history.**
  - o "Self Evident, a podcast and resource that honors the everyday lives of Asian American people." https://selfevidentshow.com/.
  - o PBS's five-part documentary series *Asian Americans* https://www.documentary.org/blog/documentaries-watch-asian-and-pacific-islander-american-heritage-month.

- o YouTube documentary series #AsianAmCovidStories, which goes in-depth on everything from the history of Asians in America to their recent experiences during the pandemic https://www.youtube.com/playlist?list= PLuH1M1754dgDjrdZJytzLw-GAJL2HYC0c.
- **Think about the training you can take to be a better ally in the workplace.**
  - o Take allyship training such as the Asian Americans Advancing Justice's Bystander Intervention Training https://www.advancingjustice-aajc.org/trainings- address-anti-asianamerican-harassment and LinkedIn Learning's Understanding and Supporting Asian Employees https://www.linkedin.com/learning/under- standing-and-supporting-asian-employees/ understanding-and-supporting-asian-employees.
- **Challenge the status quo with anti-racist resources.**
  - o https://www.catalyst.org/research/anti-racist- resources/.

12

Integrating Diversity, Equity, and Inclusion into Learning and Development

Jessalin Lam

DEI and L&D are inextricably linked. A culture of inclusion requires a culture of learning. The more that we are curious, challenge our biases, and bring diverse perspectives into the conversation, the more we are able to come up with better solutions for problems and adapt to new situations. All of this deeply impacts the success of an organization.
—Nikki Cannon, co-founder, Nclusion Works

THIS CHAPTER WILL help you understand how diversity, equity, and inclusion (DEI) relates to talent development and the importance of integrating it into learning and development (L&D) in order to help recruit and retain employees. It will discuss how to set yourself up for success when it comes to combining DEI with business goals for everyone in the organization.

Defining Diversity, Equity, and Inclusion

Diversity, *equity*, and *inclusion* are words we are hearing much more often these days, and cultivating a culture of DEI to recruit and retain talent is a challenge many organizations are facing, especially during the Great Resignation where employees are leaving their jobs or switching careers during the post-pandemic era. Let's begin by thinking about what DEI means in a simpler way. According to inclusion strategist Vernā Myers, "Diversity is being invited to the party. Inclusion is being asked to dance."[1]

To add to this, you can think about DEI like this:

- Diversity is being invited to the party. **This is a fact.**
- Equity is being on the planning committee. **This is a choice.**
- Inclusion is being asked to dance. **This is an action.**

Belonging is also a piece of the puzzle, which you can view as feeling free to dance however you want. **This is the outcome.** It is important to acknowledge all of these components, as we often forget about the outcome, which ultimately empowers people to be who they are. You cannot have one of these without the others for it to be powerful. Think about each component of your facts, choices, and actions as puzzle pieces to get to your outcome. You need to be strategic about it to create a sustainable solution, rather than picking one and being done with it. This is important for employers and leaders like yourself to consider when you are interacting with your colleagues in the workplace. Consider how your actions are making the people around you feel like they belong.

Examining the Leadership Ceiling

Let's take a look at where we are today in the corporate world for Asians in the workplace. In order to improve mobility into leadership roles for more Asian Americans, we need to understand the challenges they face.

- **Asian Americans are least likely to be promoted:** The national Equal Employment Opportunity Commission Workforce data found that Asian American professionals are the least likely group to be promoted into management—less than any other race including Blacks and Hispanics. White professionals are twice as likely to be promoted into management as their Asian American counterparts.[2]

- **Asian Americans are absent from executive roles:** Individuals of Asian descent represent 13 percent of the U.S. professional workforce but only 6 percent of executive roles, according to Ascend, a Pan-Asian, New York City–based nonprofit for business professionals. Meanwhile, white individuals represent 69 percent of the workforce but 85 percent of senior roles.[3]

- **Asian Americans face constant stereotyping:** Asian leaders must overcome stereotypes that they are considered book smart and are seen as lacking social skills or strategic thinking. Their appearance and accents often make it difficult for them to gain credibility at work.

- **Asian Americans are not being seen for who they are:** They are frequently viewed as "all Asians look the same." Colleagues confuse their Asian employees due to the way they look resulting in Asians not being seen for who they identify as.

The Asian American "bamboo ceiling" needs to be eliminated. In Chapter 9 about becoming an effective leader and manager, you briefly learned about the bamboo ceiling. Sixty-five percent of Asian American managers view the bamboo ceiling as a moderate to serious problem in their careers.[4] To break through this leadership ceiling, you can:

- **Build relationships:** Proactively reach out to people externally and internally to cultivate a strong network as a long-term investment for your career.
- **Increase your visibility:** Consider projects that make you stand out in order for your organization to see the unique value you bring to the table. Be intentional in positioning yourself as a thought leader, and apply what you learned from the chapter of building your brand to stake a claim at work.
- **Speak up more:** Ask for what you want, promote your achievements, and actively speak up. Push yourself outside your comfort zone to keep growing and moving forward.

Combining Your DEI Efforts

Let's discuss why we need to integrate DEI efforts with L&D. According to Josh Bersin's "Elevating Equity" report, 75 percent of companies do not have DEI included in the company's leadership development or overall learning and development plan, and only 32 percent of companies mandate any form of DEI training for employees.[5] In many organizations, DEI and L&D may exist in silos, which is not ideal. Instead, companies should ensure that L&D is a strategic driver to reshape and rebuild the organization to become more efficient when setting DEI business goals. Companies have an opportunity to change the future by focusing on retaining talent and integrating DEI into the conversation and business to support talent.

Here are ways to integrate DEI into your L&D strategy to set yourself up for success in the long term for talent development, especially recruiting and retaining talent. Even though you may not be the one creating this for your organization, think about how you can apply this when creating your own learning and development plan as you keep growing within your professional career. Think also about how you can support others around you by sharing these resources and creating opportunities to support a more inclusive workplace.

Participating in Mentorship Programs

You learned about the magic of mentorship in an earlier chapter; participating in mentorship programs as a mentor or mentee will support employee retainment and support career growth opportunities. Consider mentoring people from marginalized communities to help them push past barriers as they may not have the privileges that others have in the workplace. When you give them a chance by investing time to mentor them, you are also committing to their professional development and opening their minds to perspectives and ideas they may have not known existed. You can tap into industry mentorship programs that already exist externally or create your own internal programs within your organization or communities. Depending on your company's priorities, you could create mentorship programs for a specific audience. For example, the Asian American Advertising Federation (3AF) and Asians in Advertising partnered together to offer a NextGen Leaders Mentorship Program specifically for Asian American marketing professionals.

Considering Succession Planning and Leadership Programs

Invest in leadership training where you require employees to understand how to be an inclusive leader in order to get promoted to the next level. Some organizations also require employees to take unconscious bias training and learn how to interview candidates to remove barriers when recruiting people to their teams. Organizations should integrate DEI across the company for all employees to see the importance of it and tie it back into succession planning and leadership programs. Performance reviews also should align with the DEI business goals of the organization. It will speak volumes and create a bigger impact when you combine DEI goals into employee goals that affect their mindset and behavior within your organization rather than choosing check-the-box compliance training. When leaders know better and do better, that knowledge will trickle down to hiring managers and supervisors.

You can also consider creating a leadership program for your organization or tap into external resources. For example, the Advertising Club of New York created an annual i'mPART fellowship program to elevate women in mid-level positions, and the Women in Power's fellowship program provides senior-level women across all professional sectors the peer support, mentorship, training, and coaching needed to advance to the highest levels of leadership.

Enrolling in Professional Development Training

Earlier in my career, I was fortunate to be selected to participate in a Digital Acceleration workshop that provided a scholarship for thirty young marketing professionals of color organized by the Advertising Club of New York. These opportunities were truly life-changing for me. Asian American leaders must have the opportunity to participate in learning and development programs since the model minority myth often makes it seem like Asians do not need the help and are not frequently selected. Companies should consider intentionally creating training opportunities for marginalized communities and make sure to enroll in professional development training beyond leadership programs. They should take the time to invest in the professional growth of marginalized communities with resources to ensure each employee continues to thrive in their career journey. For example, companies could hire coaches for their Asian employees or offer presentation skills training. They can also share external resources or partner with organizations that will sponsor opportunities for marginalized communities.

Providing Access to Leadership

Who is in the room when you are in meetings? Are there opportunities for employees to connect with your company executives? Opportunities can be as simple as virtual coffee hours that provide employees with access to leadership to learn from them and facilitate an "ask me anything." This aligns with increasing employee engagement, retention, and visibility as well as contributing to their professional development with career opportunities to network across leaders within the organization. In addition to internal resources, you can also provide external resources for access to leaders. For example, Asians in Advertising organized a leadership speaker series as a three-part series featuring Asian leaders across entry-, mid-, and c-suite levels for them to share how they navigated their careers. This was a great career development opportunity to provide access to other industry leaders. You can easily replicate this within your own organization and communities.

Interview with Sonali Goel

Sonali Goel (she/her) is the senior director of talent and development at Macmillan. Sonali's expertise lies in partnering strategically with business leaders to define, articulate, and sustain a high-performing, inclusive culture, where people are excited to learn and do their best work. As a people practices leader, Sonali crafts and executes forward-thinking development, engagement, and retention strategies that align with company values and address immediate and emerging talent needs. Sonali is an active DEI advocate, sits on Macmillan's DEI Council, and is the executive sponsor of several Macmillan employee resource groups.

What are you doing to integrate DEI into L&D that impacts upward mobility?

We integrate DEI in multiple ways: by including examples, images, and names that are representative and inclusive; through case studies that address real workplace situations around career conversations, and planning career journeys; through mentorship and sponsorship programs; by ensuring DEI principles are part of our general programming, in addition to designing and facilitating targeted programs. Most importantly, we continuously explore ways to ensure L&D programming is equitably available and accessible to everyone in the organization.

What are your tips for how people can sustain a high-performing, inclusive culture, where people are excited to learn and do their best work?

Be intentional about the culture you want and how each employee contributes to the culture. Establish clear company values, as well as clear performance expectations. Then practice these values; check in on performance; ask for and give candid, actionable feedback. Finally, hold yourself and each other accountable for actions and results. Reward behaviors that strengthen your culture, and hold people accountable for behaviors that diminish the culture. People know when you're being performative, and doing what you said you'd do builds trust, commitment, and change.

What resources do you recommend for DEI in the workplace?

Because DEI is multilayered, with many different facets, cast your net wide when exploring resources. Some resources I find useful include employee resource groups, community-based professional organizations, and of course, as many books and articles I can find. On social media, I follow companies and individuals who champion DEI. If your company has a DEI team, or DEI champions, I highly recommend speaking with them to learn about your company's DEI initiatives, to seek guidance on DEI matters in the workplace and resources that they recommend to help you in your DEI journey.

What are the DEI challenges employers need to change for the future of the workplace?

From my perspective, the biggest challenge we need to overcome is treating DEI as a separate initiative. To truly drive change, DEI principles need to be integrated into everyday workflows and decision-making. We shouldn't have to stop and put on our "DEI hat" at certain points in a process; it should be an integral part of the process. Employers should stop thinking of DEI as a People initiative, and start thinking about it as a Business imperative.

How has being Asian affected your career?

I've navigated so many headwinds and tailwinds because I am Asian. I credit my thirst for knowledge, my ambition to succeed, my desire to prove myself, and my strong work ethic to my heritage. On the flip side, it took me many years to realize that I had to advocate for myself, that it was okay for me to challenge people more senior to me, and that being vocal and visible would help my career, rather than hinder my growth. I have been proud of being the only Asian in the room, and now take pride in mentoring and sponsoring other Asians so I am no longer the only one in the room.

Key Takeaways

- Diversity is being invited to the party, equity is being on the planning committee, inclusion is being asked to dance, and belonging is feeling free to dance however you want. You need all of these components to have the most impact.
- Some ways to integrate DEI into learning and development include participating in mentorship programs, considering leadership programs, and enrolling in training courses.

■ You can break through the leadership ceiling by building relationships, increasing your visibility, and speaking up more as you create more opportunities throughout your career.

Reflections

■ **What can you do to increase your visibility as a leader?**
  o Position yourself as a thought leader and subject matter expert to contribute your expertise at industry conferences.
  o Participate in leadership programs and fellowships to improve your leadership skills.
■ **When was the last time you invested in professional development for yourself?**
  o Make a list of training that will help you grow in your career.
■ **Are you contributing to your organization's succession planning?**
  o Since Asians are less likely to be promoted into management, ask for that raise and promotion now to put yourself higher in the hierarchy for that higher position.

Conclusion

We appreciate that you finished reading this book, and we encourage you to use this as a reference guide to go back to and apply what you have learned from each chapter to your life. We hope you share this book as a resource to those in your network, community, friends, or whomever you feel could benefit from it.

What you need to remember is that "visibility" is a mindset. Incorporating this mindset into your professional development will help you to seize the opportunities you deserve in your career. It's not about settling for how others see you but making space for others to recognize your full potential. It's about listening to your inner voice, saying, "How can I be seen? Am I showing up in the best possible way? What more can I do?" so that you're making sure you are able to bring an abundance of opportunities to your doorstep.

We recommend you review the key takeaways and assess where you are with your own visibility mindset as you create opportunities and push past barriers for yourself and your community. This book was divided into three parts: improving yourself, working with others, and redefining the future of the workplace as the key components contributing to your visibility throughout your career journey. Think about this book as your professional toolkit to equip you to flourish and thrive as an Asian American in the workplace or to help allies learning how to support our community.

When it comes to improving yourself, you are utilizing effective communication with your voice to speak up and be heard, recognizing the unique value you bring to the workplace, building a strategic personal brand, becoming a trailblazer, optimizing a healthy work-life balance, and breaking the stigma of mental health in the workplace.

As you continue to work with others on a professional level, you are learning ways to address microaggressions, creating your own networking toolkit to grow your connections, understanding leadership styles to apply, and optimizing mentorship as a mentor and mentee.

Redefining the future of the workplace is essential for the steps you take today shaping our tomorrow. As you learned in this last section, we can all be a better ally to bring forth a better future. You can apply what you learned from this book to become a more effective ally and be mindful of your leadership.

Creating a Visibility Mindset Plan

We want to make sure you have a call to action from this book by creating your own **Visibility Mindset Plan**. You can personalize the following worksheet for yourself based on what you learned from each section of this book. Answer the following questions to build your strategic plan for each area of development:

Where am I now?

- *What is your current situation?*
- *What change do you want to create?*

Where do I want to be?

- *What are your goals and dreams for each area of development?*
- *What is your ideal outcome for these in the workplace?*

How do I get there?

- *What are the essential steps you need to take to accomplish your goals?*
- *What are the action steps you can take today?*

My Visibility Mindset Plan	Where am I now?	Where do I want to be?	How do I get there?
Improving Yourself			
• Finding your own voice			
• Knowing your worth			
• Building your personal brand			
• Creating your own career path			
• Finding your optimal work-life balance			
• Prioritizing your mental health			
Working with Others			
• Addressing microaggressions			
• Maximizing the power of networking			
• Becoming an effective leader and manager			
• Optimizing the magic of mentorship			
Redefining the Future of the Workplace			
• Leveraging allyship			
• Integrating diversity, equity, and inclusion into learning and development			

Notes

Introduction

1. Clara Luo, "*A Challenge to Our Industry from an Invisible Minority*," *Campaign*, March 29, 2021. https://www. campaignlive.com/article/challenge-industry-invisible-minority/1711249
2. Connie Hanzhang Jin, "6 Charts That Dismantle the Trope of Asian Americans as a Model Minority," National Public Radio, May 25, 2021. https://www.npr.org/2021/05/25/ 999874296/6-charts-that-dismantle-the-trope-of-asian-americans-as-a-model-minority
3. Nguyen Ngan and Kim Euna, "Model Minority Myth and the Double-Edged Sword," Ascend Leadership Foundation, April 2021. https://www.ascendleadershipfoundation.org/ research/model-minority-myth-double-edged-sword
4. Rakesh Kochhar and Anthony Cilluffo, "Income Inequality in the U.S. Is Rising Most Rapidly among Asians," Pew Research Center, July 18, 2018. https://www.pewresearch .org/social-trends/2018/07/12/income-inequality-in-the-u-s-is-rising-most-rapidly-among-asians/

5. Victoria Tran, "Asian Americans Are Falling through the Cracks in Data Representation and Social Services," Urban Institute, June 19, 2018. https://www.urban.org/urban-wire/asian-americans-are-falling-through-cracks-data-representation-and-social-services

6. Agnes Constante, "Largest U.S. refugee group struggling with poverty 45 years after resettlement," NBC News, March 4, 2020. https://www.nbcnews.com/news/asian-america/largest-u-s-refugee-group-struggling-poverty-45-years-after-n1150031

7. STAATUS Index, "STAATUS Index Report 2021," 2021. https://www.staatus-index.org/staatus-index-2021

8. Barbara Frankel, "Asian Divide in the C-Suite," DiversityInc, April 13, 2022. https://www.diversityincbestpractices.com/the-asian-divide-in-the-c-suite/

Chapter 1

1. "Asian Americans Are the Least Likely Group in the U.S. to Be Promoted to Management," *Harvard Business Review*, August 31, 2021. https://hbr.org/2018/05/asian-americans-are-the-least-likely-group-in-the-u-s-to-be-promoted-to-management

2. Anemona Hartocollis, "Harvard Rated Asian-American Applicants Lower on Personality Traits, Suit Says," *New York Times*, June 15, 2018. https://www.nytimes.com/2018/06/15/us/harvard-asian-enrollment-applicants.html

3. Drake Baer, "If You Want to Get Hired, Act Like Your Potential Boss," *Business Insider*, May 29, 2014. https://www.businessinsider.com/managers-hire-people-who-remind-them-of-themselves-2014-5

4. Carol Kinsey Goman, "The Art and Science of Mirroring," *Forbes*, June 25, 2011. https://www.forbes.com/sites/carolkinseygoman/2011/05/31/the-art-and-science-of-mirroring/?sh=3ed83f731318

5. Kristin Wong, "Boost Your Professional Reputation by Always Showing up Five Minutes Early," Lifehacker, October 15, 2015. https://lifehacker.com/boost-your-professional-reputation-by-always-showing-up-173662 1526

Chapter 2

1. Jerald G. Bachman, Patrick M. O'Malley, Peter Freedman-Doan, Kali H. Trzesniewski, and M. Brent Donnellan, "Adolescent Self-Esteem: Differences by Race/Ethnicity, Gender, and Age," National Center of Medicine, National Center for Biotechnology Information, January 23, 2011. https://www.ncbi.nlm.nih.gov/pmc/articles/PMC 3263756/
2. "The Rise of Asian Americans," Pew Research Center, June 19, 2012. https://www.pewresearch.org/social-trends/2012/06/19/the-rise-of-asian-americans/
3. Sylvia Rani, "Addressing Impostor Syndrome," University of Minnesota, 2016. https://www.takingcharge.csh.umn.edu/addressing-impostor-syndrome2
4. "The State of the Gender Pay Gap in 2021," Payscale, 2021. https://www.payscale.com/research-and-insights/gender-pay-gap/

Chapter 3

1. Alia Wong, "Why Whites and Asians Have Different Views on Personal Success," *The Atlantic*, July 20, 2017. https://www.theatlantic.com/education/archive/2017/07/whites-asians-personal-success/534237/
2. Goldie Chan, "10 Golden Rules of Personal Branding," *Forbes*, December 10, 2021. https://www.forbes.com/sites/goldiechan/2018/11/08/10-golden-rules-personal-branding/?sh=6f1fb5ed58a7

Chapter 4

1. "Workforce Transitions: A Tale of Career Pivots," *The Colorado Springs Business Journal*, 2021. https://www.csbj.com/premier/businessnews/workforce-transitions-a-tale-of-career-pivots-part-2/article_ed2053b8-b913-56a6-bda5-9991ea8c2e3a.html
2. "Pivoting Your Career and Switching Fields," NAAAP DC—National Association of Asian American Professionals, 2021. https://www.facebook.com/NAAAPDC/videos/pivoting-your-career-and-switching-fields/933034070594000/
3. Cynthia Pong, *Don't Stay in Your Lane: The Career Change Guide for Women of Color* (New York: Embrace Change Consulting LLC), August 27, 2020

Chapter 5

1. OECD, "Employment - Hours Worked - OECD Data," 2019. https://data.oecd.org/emp/hours-worked.htm
2. World Health Organization, "Long Working Hours Increasing Deaths from Heart Disease and Stroke: WHO, ILO," World Health Organization, May 17, 2021. www.who.int/news/item/17-05-2021-long-working-hours-increasing-deaths-from-heart-disease-and-stroke-who-ilo
3. Ana Sandoiu, "Poor Work-Life Balance Leads to Poor Health Later in Life," Medical News Today, October 29, 2016. www.medicalnewstoday.com/articles/313755
4. Bureau of Labor Statistics, "American Time Use Survey Activity Lexicon," 2012. Retrieved March 2, 2015 from: http://www.bls.gov/tus/lexiconwex2012.pdf

Chapter 6

1. World Health Organization, "Mental Health: Strengthening Our Response," *World Health Organization*, March 30, 2018.

www.who.int/en/news-room/fact-sheets/detail/mental-health-strengthening-our-response

2. Asian American Psychological Association Leadership Fellows Program, "Suicide among Asian Americans: Myths about Suicides among Asian Americans," American Psychological Association, January 2012. www.apa.org/pi/oema/resources/ethnicity-health/asian-american/suicide

3. Ryann Tanap, "Why Asian-Americans and Pacific Islanders Don't Go to Therapy," National Alliance on Mental Illness, July 25, 2019. www.nami.org/Blogs/NAMI-Blog/July-2019/Why-Asian-Americans-and-Pacific-Islanders-Don-t-go-to-Therapy

4. Substance Abuse and Mental Health Services Administration, "Racial/Ethnic Differences in Mental Health Service Use among Adults," HHS Publication No. SMA-15-4906 (Rockville, Md.: Substance Abuse and Mental Health Services Administration, 2015). https://www.samhsa.gov/data/sites/default/files/MHServicesUseAmongAdults/MHServicesUseAmongAdults.pdf

5. Milja Milenkovic, "42 Worrying Workplace Stress Statistics," American Institute of Stress, September 23, 2019. www.stress.org/42-worrying-workplace-stress-statistics

6. The American Institute of Stress, "40+ Worrisome Workplace Stress Statistics 2022: Facts, Causes, and Trends," 2022. https://www.stress.org/workplace-stress

Chapter 7

1. Jillesa Gebhardt, "Study: Microaggressions in the Workplace," SurveyMonkey. Accessed June 8, 2022. https://www.surveymonkey.com/curiosity/microaggressions-research/

2. Derald Wing Sue, "What Is a Microaggression? What to Know about These Everyday Slights," NewYork-Presbyterian, December 10, 2020. https://healthmatters.nyp.org/what-to-know-about-microaggressions/

3. Dartmouth.edu, "The Malleable Yet Undying Nature of the Yellow Peril," 2019. https://www.dartmouth.edu/~hist32/History/S22%20The%20Malleable%20Yet%20Undying%20Nature%20of%20the%20Yellow%20Peril.htm

4. John Cho, "John Cho: Coronavirus Reminds Asian Americans Belonging Is Conditional," *Los Angeles Times*, April 22, 2020. https://www.latimes.com/opinion/story/2020-04-22/asian-american-discrimination-john-cho-coronavirus

5. Warren Ng, "'Death by a Thousand Cuts': The Impact of Microaggressions on the AAPI Community," NewYork-Presbyterian, May 25, 2021. https://healthmatters.nyp.org/death-by-a-thousand-cuts-the-impact-of-microaggressions-on-the-aapi-community/

6. Aggie J. Yellow Horse, Russell Jeung, and Ronae Matriano, "Stop AAPI Hate National Report (through September 2021)," Stop AAPI Hate, November 18, 2021. https://stopaapihate.org/national-report-through-september-2021/

7. Derald Wing Sue, "Racial Microaggressions and the Asian American Experience," *Cultural Diversity & Ethnic Minority Psychology*, U.S. National Library of Medicine. Accessed June 8, 2022. https://pubmed.ncbi.nlm.nih.gov/17227179/

8. Anne Saw, Aggie J. Yellow Horse, and Russell Jeung, "Stop AAPI Hate Mental Health Report," Stop AAPI Hate, May 27, 2021. https://stopaapihate.org/mental-health-report/

9. "Asian American/Pacific Islander Communities and Mental Health," Mental Health America. Accessed June 8, 2022. https://www.mhanational.org/issues/asian-americanpacific-islander-communities-and-mental-health

10. Jennifer Lu and Ada Tseng, "Verbal Jiujitsu, Disarming and Other Tips for Dealing with Microaggressions," *Los Angeles*

Times, June 2, 2021. unacceptable%20behavior%2C%E2%80%9D%20Sue%20said

11. Ella F. Washington, Alison Hall Birch, and Laura Morgan Roberts, "When and How to Respond to Microaggressions," *Harvard Business Review*, July 3, 2020. https://hbr.org/2020/07/when-and-how-to-respond-to-microaggressions

12. Rubin Thomlinson, "How Do I Respond to a Microaggression?" *Lexology*, July 7, 2020. https://www.lexology.com/library/detail.aspx?g=cb90395a-4293-4927-961c-12c103b2d24a

Chapter 8

1. Sallie Krawcheck, "Sallie Krawcheck Reveals the #1 Unwritten Rule of Success," *HuffPost*, September 17, 2013. https://www.huffpost.com/entry/sallie-krawcheck_n_3937342

2. Julia Freeland Fisher, "How to Get a Job Often Comes Down to One Elite Personal Asset, and Many People Still Don't Realize It," CNBC, December 27, 2019. https://www.cnbc.com/2019/12/27/how-to-get-a-job-often-comes-down-to-one-elite-personal-asset.html

3. Bianca Miller Cole, "10 Reasons Why Networking Is Essential for Your Career," *Forbes*, March 20, 2019. https://www.forbes.com/sites/biancamillercole/2019/03/20/why-networking-should-be-at-the-core-of-your-career/?sh=31c899de1300

4. Jenny Chang, "45 Significant Business Networking Statistics: 2022 Conversion Rates & Challenges," Finances Online, 2022. https://financesonline.com/business-networking-statistics/

5. Dr. David Mee-Lee, "Understanding Cultural Differences: Asian Culture," *Care Compass Network*, January 29, 2018. https://carecompassnetwork.org/understanding-cultural-differences-asian-culture/

6. Hanne Keiling, "4 Types of Communication and How to Improve Them," *Indeed*, May 25, 2022. https://www .indeed.com/career-advice/career-development/types-of-communication

7. Rose Leadeam, "The Art and Science of Networking (Infographic)," *Entrepreneur*, April 28, 2018. https://www .entrepreneur.com/article/312600

Chapter 9

1. Stefanie K. Johnson and Thomas Sy, "Why Aren't There More Asian Americans in Leadership Positions?" *Harvard Business Review*, December 19, 2016. hbr.org/2016/12/ why-arent-there-more-asian-americans-in-leadership-positions

2. Buck Gee and Denise Peck, "Asian Americans Are the Least Likely Group in the U.S. to Be Promoted to Management," *Harvard Business Review*, May 31, 2018. hbr.org/2018/05/ asian-americans-are-the-least-likely-group-in-the-u-s-to-be-promoted-to-management

3. Randall J. Beck and Jim Harter, "Why Great Managers Are so Rare." Gallup.com. *Gallup*, October 22, 2018. https:// www.gallup.com/workplace/231593/why-great-managers-rare.aspx

4. Ibid.

5. Thomas Oppong, "6 Habits of People Who Actively Embrace Their Vulnerability," *Thrive Global*, March 12, 2020. thriveglobal.com/stories/embrace-vulnerability-how-to-habits-personal-growth/

6. Jackson G. Lu et al., "Why East Asians but Not South Asians Are Underrepresented in Leadership Positions in the United States," *PNAS*, February 18, 2020. www.pnas .org/doi/10.1073/pnas.1918896117

Chapter 10

1. Lisa Quast, "How Becoming a Mentor Can Boost Your Career," *Forbes*, August 21, 2012. https://www.forbes.com/sites/lisaquast/2011/10/31/how-becoming-a-mentor-can-boost-your-career/?sh=1f14779c5f57

Chapter 11

1. Joanne Dias, "What Is Allyship?" Center for Creative Leadership, February 19, 2021. www.ccl.org/articles/leading-effectively-articles/what-is-allyship-your-questions-answered/
2. Ibid.
3. Katy Steinmetz, "She Coined the Term 'Intersectionality' over 30 Years Ago. Here's What It Means to Her Today," *Time*, February 20, 2020. time.com/5786710/kimberle-crenshaw-intersectionality/

Chapter 12

1. Laura Sherbin and Ripa Rashid, "Diversity Doesn't Stick without Inclusion," *Harvard Business Review*, February 17, 2017. hbr.org/2017/02/diversity-doesnt-stick-without-inclusion
2. Buck Gee and Denise Peck, "Asian Americans Are the Least Likely Group in the U.S. to Be Promoted to Management," *Harvard Business Review*, May 13, 2018. https://hbr.org/2018/05/asian-americans-are-the-least-likely-group-in-the-u-s-to-be-promoted-to-management
3. Theresa Agovino, "Asian-Americans Seek More Respect, Authority in the Workplace," *SHRM*, June 19, 2021. www.shrm.org/hr-today/news/all-things-work/pages/asian-americans-in-the-workplace.aspx

4. Association of Asian American Investment Managers (AAAIM), "Good Workers—Not Leaders: Unconscious Biases That Stall AAPI Advancement," *Association of Asian American Investment Managers (AAAIM)*, September 21, 2021. aaaim.org/goodworkers-notleaders/

5. Josh Bersin, "Elevating Equity and Diversity: The Challenge of the Decade," Josh Bersin, February 11, 2021. joshbersin .com/2021/02/elevating-equity-and-diversity-the-challenge-of-the-decade/

Index